MEDITERRANEAN DIET 2020 FOR BEGINNERS

100 QUick- easy anD eveRyDay cooking healThy way Recipes- a cookBook.

B Y

STEF HARRISON

©Copyright 2019by STEF HARRISON

All rights reserved.This document is geared towards providing exact and reliable information with regards to the topic and issue covered. The publication is sold with the idea that the publisher is not required to render accounting, officially permitted, or otherwise, qualified services. If advice is necessary, legal or professional, a practiced individual in the profession should be ordered. -From a Declaration of Principles which was accepted and approved equally by a Committee of the American Bar Association and a Committee of Publishers and Associations. In no way is it legal to reproduce, duplicate, or transmit any part of this document in either electronic means or in printed format. Recording of this publication is strictly prohibited and any storage of this document is not allowed unless with written permission from the publisher. All rights reserved. The information provided herein is stated to be truthful and consistent, in that any liability, in terms of inattention or otherwise, by any usage or abuse of any policies, processes, or directions contained within is the solitary and utter responsibility of the recipient reader. Under no circumstances will any legal responsibility or blame be held against the publisher for any reparation, damages, or monetary loss due to the information herein, either directly or indirectly. Respective authors own all copyrights not held by the publisher. The information herein is offered for informational purposes solely, and is universal as so. The presentation of the information is without contract or any type of guarantee assurance. The trademarks that are used are without any consent, and the publication of the trademark is without permission or backing by the trademark owner. All trademarks and brands within this book are for clarifying purposes only and are the owned by the owners themselves, not affiliated with this document.

Contents

Feta Garbanzo Bean Salad 13
Cod and Asparagus Bake 15
Salmon with Spinach & White Beans 17
Skillet Chicken with Olives 19
Mediterranean Pork and Orzo 21
Elegant Pork Marsala 23
Pesto Corn Salad with Shrimp 26
Bruschetta Steak 28
Grilled Salmon with Nectarines 30
Tomato-Garlic Lentil Bowls 32
Mediterranean Turkey Skillet 34
Chicken Thighs with Shallots & Spinach 36
Balsamic-Glazed Beef Skewers 38
Pronto Vegetarian Peppers 40
Mediterranean Chickpeas 42
Rosemary Chicken with Spinach & Beans 44
Skillet Beef and Potatoes 46
Lemon-Lime Salmon with Veggie Saute 48
Tuscan Chicken and Beans 51
Mediterranean Tilapia 53
California Quinoa 55
Salmon with Root Vegetables 57
Mediterranean Chicken Stir-Fry 59
Stuffed-Olive Cod 61
Tuna and White Bean Lettuce Wraps 63
Whole Wheat Orzo Salad 65
Garden Quinoa Salad 67

Mahi Mahi & Veggie Skillet 69
Lemon-Olive Chicken with Orzo..71
Blackened Tilapia with Zucchini Noodles 73
Sweet-Chili Salmon with Blackberries................................ 75
Arugula & Brown Rice Salad 77
Sauteed Pork Chops with Garlic Spinach 79
Warm Rice & Pintos Salad 82
Chicken & Goat Cheese Skillet..84
Lemon Salmon with Basil 86
Greek Fish Bake 88
Caesar Salmon with Roasted Tomatoes & Artichokes 90
Citrus Scallops... 92
Quinoa-Stuffed Squash Boats 94
Grapefruit-Gremolata Salmon... 96
Cod with Bacon & Balsamic Tomatoes 98
Pizzaiola Chops 100
Garlic Tilapia with Spicy Kale.. 102
Pepper and Salsa Cod... 104
Peppered Tuna Kabobs 106
Tomato-Herb Grilled Tilapia 108
Chili-Rubbed Steak with Black Bean Salad 110
Salmon Veggie Packets..114
Tomato-Poached Halibut.. 117
Pistachio Salmon...119
Creamy Lentils with Kale Artichoke Saute.................... 121
Ginger Salmon with Green Beans 124
Pan-Seared Cod..127
Kale-and-Chickpea Grain Bowl with Avocado Dressing ... 129
Quick Chicken Marsala 132
Shrimp and Leek Spaghetti..135

Simple Mediterranean Olive Oil Pasta 138
Homemade Chicken Shawarma 141
Greek Tzatziki Sauce Recipe...144
One-pan Mediterranean Baked Halibut Recipe with
Vegetables 146
Greek Chicken Souvlaki..149
Greek Roasted Potatoes 153
Easy Mediterranean Shrimp Recipe....................................155
Garlic Dijon Chicken..158
Traditional Greek Salad...161
Moroccan Vegetable Tagine..164
Mediterranean Watermelon Salad 167
Mediterranean Roasted Leg of Lamb 169
Kofta Kebabs 176
Lebanese Rice..179
Mediterranean Stuffed Peppers..182
Moroccan Lamb Stew 185
How to Make the Best Diner-Style Greek Salad...................188
Light & Fresh Italian Pasta Salad 190
Greek-Style Tuna Salad...192
Baked Red Lentil Falafel Salad 194
Warm Pasta Salad With Tomatoes and Eggplant 198
Grilled Heirloom Tomato and Feta Panzanella 201
Zucchini-Pesto-Sausage Pizza 203
Chicken and Cucumber Salad With Parsley Pesto..............206
Gnocchi With Spinach and Pepper Sauce 209
Extra-Crispy Veggie-Packed Pizza......................................211
Chicken and Bulgur Salad With Peaches 214
Spring Salad With Herbed Goat Cheese..............................217

If you're searching for a heart-good dieting arrangement, the Mediterranean diet may be for you. The Mediterranean diet mixes the fundamentals of good dieting with the traditional flavors and cooking methods of the Mediterranean.

Why the Mediterranean diet?

Enthusiasm for the Mediterranean diet started during the 1960s with the perception that coronary illness caused fewer deaths in Mediterranean countries such as Greece and Italy than in the U.S. or northern Europe. Resultss found that the Mediterranean diet is related to diminished risk factors for cardiovascular issues.

The Mediterranean eating routine is one of the dieting plans prescribed by the Dietary Guidelines for Americans to advance wellbeing and prevent chronic diseases.

It is additionally perceived by the World Health Organization as a healthy and feasible dietary example and as an intangible cultural resource by the United National Educational, Scientific and Cultural Organization.

What is the Mediterranean diet?

The Mediterranean eating regimen is a way for eating dependent on the traditional cuisine of countries flanking the Mediterranean Sea. While there is no single meaning of the

Mediterranean diet, it is ordinarily high in vegetables, fruits, whole grains, beans, nut and seeds, and olive oil.

The primary components of Mediterranean eating routine add:

- Every day utilization of vegetables, natural products, whole grains and solid fats
- Week by week intake of fish, poultry, beans and eggs
- Moderate parts of dairy products
- Limited intake of red meat

Other significant components of the Mediterranean diet are imparting meals to loved ones, getting a charge out of a glass of red wine and being physically active.

Plant-based, not meat-based

The establishment of the Mediterranean eating routine is vegetables, organic products, herbs, nuts, beans, and whole grains. Meals are worked around these plant-based foods. Moderate measures of dairy, poultry, and eggs are additionally fundamental to the Mediterranean Diet, as is seafood.

Healthy fats

Healthy fats are a pillar of the Mediterranean eating regimen. They're eaten rather than less solid fats, for example, saturated and Trans fats, which add to coronary disease.

Olive oil is the essential source of fat in the Mediterranean eating regimen. Olive oil gives monounsaturated fat, which has been found to bring down total cholesterol and low-density lipoprotein (LDL or "terrible") cholesterol levels. Nuts and seeds likewise contain monounsaturated fat.

Fish are additionally significant in the Mediterranean eating routine. Fatty fish — mackerel, herring, sardines, tuna fish, salmon and lake trout — are wealthy in omega-3 unsaturated fats, a kind of polyunsaturated fat that may decrease inflammation in the body. Omega-3 unsaturated fats likewise help decrease triglycerides, lessen blood clotting, and decline the risk of stroke and cardiovascular breakdown.

What about wine?

The Mediterranean eating routine normally permits red wine with some restraint. Although alcohol has been related to a decreased risk of coronary illness in certain investigations, consuming wine is not risk-free. The Dietary Guidelines for Americans caution against starting to drink or drinking all the more regularly based on potential medical advantages.

Eating the Mediterranean way

Interested in attempting the Mediterranean eating routine? These tips wil`l assist you i the beginning:

- **Eat more fruits and vegetables.** Go for 7 to 10 servings every day of products of the soil.
- **Select whole grains.** Change to whole grain bread, oats, and pasta. Examination with other whole grains, for example, bulgur and farro.
- **Eat more seafood.** Eat fish two times per week. Crisp or water-stuffed fish, salmon, trout, mackerel, and herring are solid decisions. Grilled fish tastes great and requires little cleanup. Maintain a strategic distance from deep-fried fish.
- **Decrease red meat.** Substitute fish, poultry or beans for meat. If you eat meat, ensure its lean and keep partitions little.
- **Appreciate some dairy.** Eat low-fat Greek or plain yogurt and small quantities of a variety of cheeses.
- **Zest-it up.** Herbs and flavors support to enhance and decrease the requirement for salt.

The Mediterranean eating regimen is a scrumptious approach to eat. Numerous individuals who change to this style of eating state they'll never eat some other way.

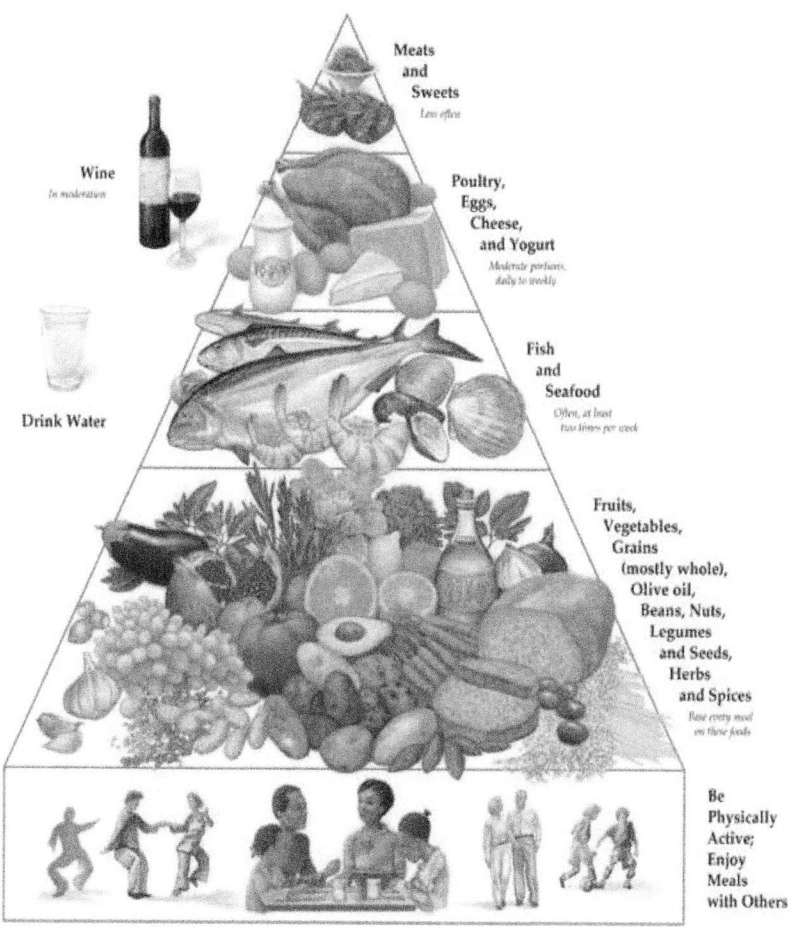

When you consider Mediterranean food, your mind may go to pizza and pasta from Italy, or lamb chops from Greece, however, these dishes don't fit into the solid dietary plans publicized as "Mediterranean." A genuine Mediterranean eating regimen depends on the district's traditional organic products, vegetables, beans, nuts, fish, olive oil, and dairy—with maybe a glass or two of red wine. Furthermore, the real

Mediterranean eating regimen is about something beyond eating crisp, healthy food. Day by day, physical activity and offering meals to others are crucial components of the Mediterranean Diet Pyramid. Together, they can profoundly affect your mindset and mental well-being and assist you with cultivating profound gratefulness for the delights of eating well and longer life.

Making changes to your eating regimen is once in a while simple, particularly in case you're attempting to move away from the accommodation of prepared and takeout foods. However, the Mediterranean eating regimen can be a modest just as a fantastic and sound approach to eating. Changing from pepperoni and pasta to fish and avocados may require some exertion, however, you could before long be on the way to a more advantageous and longer life.

Health benefits of a Mediterranean diet

A traditional Mediterranean eating routine comprising of large amounts of fresh fruits and vegetables, nuts, fish and olive oil—combined with a physical action—can diminish your risk of serious mental and physical medical issues by:

Preventing coronary disease and strokes. Following a Mediterranean eating regimen constrains your intake of refined bread, prepared foods, and red meat, and empowers drinking red wine rather than hard alcohol—all factors that can help avert coronary disease and stroke.

You are diminishing the risk of Alzheimer's. The research proposes that the Mediterranean eating routine may improve cholesterol, glucose levels, and overall blood vessel wellbeing, which like this may diminish your risk of Alzheimer's ailment or dementia.

Splitting the risk of Parkinson's disease. The significant levels of antioxidants in the Mediterranean eating routine can keep cells from experiencing a damaging process called oxidative stress, accordingly cutting the risk of Parkinson's illness into equal parts.

You are expanding longevity. By diminishing your risk of creating coronary disease or malignancy with the Mediterranean eating regimen, you're lessening your risk of death at any age by 20%.

You are protecting against type 2 diabetes. A Mediterranean eating routine is wealthy in fiber which processes gradually, forestalls tremendous swings in glucose, and can assist you with keeping up a healthy weight.

Myths and facts about the Mediterranean diet

Following Mediterranean eating, the routine has numerous advantages, yet there are still many misconceptions on precisely how to exploit the way of life to lead a more advantageous, longer life. Coming up next are a few myths and realities about the Mediterranean eating regimen.

Myth 1: It costs a great deal to eat along these lines.

Fact: If you're making meals out of beans or lentils as your fundamental wellspring of protein, and staying with generally plants and whole grains, at that point, the Mediterranean eating routine is more affordable than serving dishes of bundled or processed foods.

Myth 2: If one glass of wine is useful for your heart, at that point, three glasses is multiple times as healthy.

Fact: Moderate measures of red wine (one beverage daily for women; two for men) unquestionably has one of a kind medical advantages for your heart, yet drinking a lot of has the contrary impact. Anything over two glasses of wine can be bad for your heart.

Myth 3: Eating large dishes of pasta and bread is the Mediterranean way.

Truth: Typically, the Mediterranean people don't eat a large plate of pasta how Americans do. Rather, pasta is generally a side dish with around a 1/2-cup to 1-cup serving size. The remainder of their plate is comprised of servings of mixed greens, vegetables, fish or a little bit of natural, grass-fed meat, and maybe one cut of bread.

Myth 4: The Mediterranean eating regimen is just about food.

Fact: The food is an immense piece of the eating routine, truly, yet don't ignore different ways the Mediterranean live their lives. At the point when they plunk down for a meal, they don't sit before a TV or eat in a rush; they plunk down for a casual, leisurely meal with others, which might be similarly as significant for your wellbeing as what is on your plate. The Mediterranean additionally appreciate a lot of physical activity.

How to make the change?

In case you're feeling daunted by the idea of changing your dietary patterns to a Mediterranean eating regimen, here are a few proposals to kick you off:

Eat lots of vegetables. Attempt a straightforward plate of sliced tomatoes showered with olive oil and disintegrated feta cheese, or burden your slim outside layer pizza with peppers and mushrooms rather than sausage and pepperoni. Servings of mixed greens, soups, and crudité platters are likewise incredible approaches to load up on vegetables.

Continuously have breakfast. Natural products, whole grains, and other fiber-rich foods are an extraordinary method to begin your day, keeping you agreeably full for a considerable length of time.

Eat seafood times per week. Fish, for example, fish, salmon, herring, sablefish (dark cod), and sardines are wealthy in Omega-3 unsaturated fats, and shellfish like mussels, oysters, and mollusks have comparable advantages for the mind and heart wellbeing.

Cook a vegetarian meal one night seven days. If it's useful, you can bounce on the "Meatless Mondays" pattern of previous meat on the primary day of the week, or essentially pick a day where you assemble dinners around beans, whole grains, and vegetables. When you get its hang, attempt two evenings per week.

Appreciate dairy products in moderation. The USDA prescribes constraining immersed fat to close to 10% of your everyday calories (around 200 calories for a great many people). That still enables you to appreciate dairy products, for example, regular (natural) cheese, Greek or plain yogurt.

For dessert, eat fresh fruit. Rather than a dessert, cake or other baked goods, choose strawberries, fresh figs, grapes, or apples.

Make mealtimes a social experience

The straightforward demonstration of conversing with a friend or adored over the dinner table can assume a major role in diminishing stress and boosting state of mind. Eating with others can likewise avert indulging, making it as solid for your waistline all things considered for your standpoint. Switch off the TV and PC, set away your cell phone, and associate with somebody over a meal.

Assemble the family and keep awake to date with one another's day by day lives. Regular family meals give comfort to kids and are an extraordinary method to screen their dietary patterns also.

Offer dinners with others to grow your social network. If you live alone, cook some extra and welcome a friend, collaborator, or neighbor to go along with you.

Cook with others. Welcome a friend to share shopping and cooking obligations regarding a Mediterranean meal. Cooking with others can be a fun method to develop relationships and parting the costs can make it less expensive for both of you.

Quick start to a Mediterranean diet

The most straightforward approach to roll out the improvement to a Mediterranean eating routine is, to begin with, small steps. You can do this by:

- Sautéing food in olive oil rather than butter.
- Eating more foods grown from the ground by getting a charge out of serving of mixed greens as a starter or

side dish, snacking on the organic product, and adding veggies to different dishes.
- picking whole grains rather than refined bread, rice, and pasta.
- Subbing fish for red meat, at any rate, two times seven days.
- Farthest point high-fat dairy by changing to skim or 1% milk from 2% or whole milk

100 Quick- Easy And Everyday Cooking Healthy Way Recipes

Feta Garbanzo Bean Salad

Ingredients

- One can (15 ounces) garbanzo beans, rinsed and drained
- 1-1/2 cups coarsely sliced English cucumber

- 1 can (2-1/4 ounces) sliced ripe olives
- 1 tomato, seeded and sliced
- 1/4 cup cut red onion
- 1/4 cup sliced fresh parsley
- 3 tablespoons olive oil
- 1 tablespoon lemon juice
- 1/4 teaspoon salt
- 1/8 teaspoon pepper
- 5 cups torn mixed serving of mixed greens
- 1/2 cup feta cheese

Nutritional facts

2 cups: 268 calories, 16g fat (3g saturated fat), 8mg cholesterol, 586mg sodium, 24g starch

(4g sugars, 7g fiber), 9g protein. Diabetic Exchanges: 3 fat, 1 starch, 1 lean meat, 1 vegetable.

Cod and Asparagus Bake

Ingredients

- 4 cod filets (4 ounces each)
- 1 pound crisp thin asparagus, cut
- 1-pint cherry tomatoes, halved.
- 2 tablespoons lemon juice
- 1-1/2 teaspoons lemon zest
- 1/4 cup ground Romano cheese

Directions

- Preheat oven to 375°. cod and asparagus in a 15x10x1-in. Preparing container brushed with oil. Add tomatoes, chop sides down. Brush fish with lemon juice; sprinkle with lemon zest. Sprinkle fish and vegetables with Romano cheese. Prepare until fish starts to chip effectively with a fork, around 12 minutes.
- Remove pan from stove; preheat grill. Cook cod blend 3-4 in. from heat until vegetables are delicately browned, 2-3 minutes.

Test Kitchen tips

- If asparagus isn't in season, crisp green beans make a fine substitute and will cook in about a similar measure of time.
- We tried cod filets that were around 3/4 in. thick. You'll have to alter the preparing time up or down if your filets are thicker or thinner.

Nutritional Facts

1 serving: 141 calories, 3g fat (2g immersed fat), 45mg cholesterol, 184mg sodium, 6g starch (3g sugars, 2g fiber), 23g protein. Diabetic exchanges: 3 lean meat, 1 vegetable.

Salmon with Spinach & White Beans

Ingredients

- 4 salmon filets (4 ounces each)
- 2 teaspoons in addition to 1 tablespoon olive oil
- 1 teaspoon fish flavoring
- 1 garlic clove, minced
- 1 can (15 ounces) cannellini beans, rinsed

- 1/4 teaspoon salt
- 1/4 teaspoon pepper
- 1 bundle (8 ounces) fresh spinach
- Lemon wedges

Directions

- Preheat grill. Rub fillets with 2 teaspoons oil; sprinkle with fish. On a lubed rack of an oven skillet. Cook 5-6 in. from heat 6-8 minutes or until fish starts to flake effectively with a fork.
- Then, in a large skillet, heat remaining oil over medium warmth. Add garlic; cook 15-30 seconds or until fragrant. Add beans, salt, and pepper, blending to cover beans with garlic oil. Mix in spinach until shriveled. Serve salmon with spinach blend and lemon wedges.

Nutritional Facts

1 filet with 1/2 cup spinach mixture: 317 calories, 17g fat (3g soaked fat), 57mg cholesterol, 577mg sodium, 16g starch (0 sugars, 5g fiber), 24g protein. Diabetic Exchanges: 3 lean meat, 2 vegetable, 1 fat, 1/2 starch.

Skillet Chicken with Olives

Ingredients

- 4 boneless skinless chicken thighs (around 1 pound each)
- 1 teaspoon dried rosemary, crushed
- 1/2 teaspoon pepper
- 1/4 teaspoon salt
- 1 tablespoon olive oil

- 1/2 cup pimiento-stuffed olives, coarsely halved
- 1/4 cup white wine or chicken stock
- 1 tablespoon capers, optional

Directions

- Sprinkle chicken with rosemary, pepper, and salt. In a large skillet, heat oil over medium-high warmth. Brown chicken on both sides.
- Add olives, wine and capers. Reduce heat; stew, covered, 2-3 minutes or until a thermometer embedded in chicken reads 170°.

Nutrition Facts

1 serving (determined without capers): 237 calories, 15g fat (3g soaked fat), 76mg cholesterol, 571mg sodium, 2g starch (0 sugars, 0 fiber), and 21g protein. Diabetic Exchanges: 3 lean meat, 2 fat.

Mediterranean Pork and Orzo

Ingredients

- 1-1/2 pounds pork tenderloin
- 1 teaspoon ground pepper
- 2 tablespoons olive oil
- 3 quarts water
- 1-1/4 cups uncooked orzo pasta

- 1/4 teaspoon salt
- 1 bundle (6 ounces) fresh baby spinach
- 1 cup grape tomatoes, split
- 3/4 cup feta cheese

Directions

- Rub pork with pepper; cut into 1-in. squares. In a large nonstick skillet, heat oil over medium heat. Add pork; cook and mix until never again pink, 8-10 minutes.
- In the meantime, in a stove, heat water to the point of boiling. Mix in orzo and salt; cook, uncovered, 8 minutes. Mix in spinach; cook until orzo is delicate and spinach is withered, 45-60 seconds longer. Drain.
- Add tomatoes to pork; heat through. Mix in orzo mixture and cheese.

Nutrition Facts

1-1 /3 cups: 372 calories, 11g fat (4g immersed fat), 71mg cholesterol, 306mg sodium, 34g starch (2g sugars, 3g fiber), and 31g protein. Diabetic Exchanges: 3 lean meat, 2 starch, 1 vegetable, 1 fat.

Elegant Pork Marsala

Ingredients

- 1/3 cup whole wheat flour
- 1/2 teaspoon pepper
- 6 boneless pork midsection cuts (4 ounces each)
- 1 tablespoon olive oil
- 2 cups cut fresh mushrooms

- 1/3 cup chopped onion
- 2 turkey bacon strips, chopped
- 1/4 teaspoon minced garlic
- 1 cup Marsala wine or extra reduced sodium chicken broth
- 5 teaspoons cornstarch
- 2/3 cup low sodium chicken broth

Directions

- In a shallow bowl, blend flour and pepper. Dip pork slashes in flour blend to cover the two sides; shake off excess.
- In a large nonstick skillet covered with cooking spray, heat oil over medium warmth. Add pork cleaves; cook 4-5 minutes on each side or until a thermometer read 145°. Remove from dish; keep warm.
- In the same skillet, add mushrooms, onion and bacon to drippings; cook and mix 2-3 minutes or until mushrooms are delicate. Add garlic; cook brief longer. Add wine; increment warmth to medium-high. Cook, blending to slacken browned bits from the container.
- In a small bowl, blend cornstarch and soup until smooth; add to the container. Heat to the point of boiling; cook and mix 2 minutes or until marginally thickened. Present with pork.

Nutrition Facts

1 pork chop with 1/3 cup sauce: 232 calories, 10g fat (3g immersed fat), 60mg cholesterol, 161mg sodium, 7g starch (2g sugars, 1g fiber), 24g protein. Diabetic Exchanges: 3 lean meat, 1/2 starch, 1/2 fat.

Pesto Corn Salad with Shrimp

Ingredients

- 4 medium ears sweet corn, husked
- 1/2 cup stuffed fresh basil leaves
- 1/4 cup olive oil
- 1/2 teaspoon salt
- 1-1/2 cups cherry tomatoes halved
- 1/8 teaspoon pepper
- 1 medium ripe avocado, peeled and chopped

- 1 pound uncooked shrimp (31-40 for each pound), peeled and deveined

Directions

- In a pot of bubbling water, cook corn until tender, around 5 minutes. Drain; cool slightly. In the processor, in a food processor, beat basil, oil and 1/4 teaspoon salt until mixed.
- Cut corn from cob and spot in a bowl. Mix in tomatoes, pepper and staying salt. Add avocado and 2 tablespoons basil mixture; toss tenderly to combine.
- Thread shrimp onto metal or splashed wooden sticks; brush with residual basil mixture. Grill broil, covered, over medium warmth until shrimp turn pink, 2-4 minutes for each side. Remove shrimp from sticks; present with corn mixture.

Nutritional Facts

1 serving: 371 calories, 22g fat (3g immersed fat), 138mg cholesterol, 450mg sodium, 25g starch (8g sugars, 5g fiber), 23g protein.

Bruschetta Steak

Ingredients

- 3 medium tomatoes, cut
- 3 tablespoons minced fresh basil
- 3 tablespoons chopped fresh parsley
- 2 tablespoons olive oil
- 1 teaspoon minced crisp oregano or 1/2 teaspoon dried oregano
- 1 garlic clove, minced
- 3/4 teaspoon salt

- 1 beef flat iron or top sirloin steak (1 pound), cut into four portions
- 1/4 teaspoon pepper
- Ground Parmesan cheese

Directions

- Combine initial six ingredients; mix in 1/4 teaspoon salt.
- Sprinkle beef with pepper and staying salt. Flame broil, covered, over medium warmth or broil 4 in. from heat until meat arrives at wanted doneness (for medium-rare, a thermometer should peruse 135°; medium, 140°), 4-6 minutes for every side. Top with tomato mixture. Whenever wanted, sprinkle with cheese.

Nutritional Facts

1 steak with 1/2 cup tomato mixture: 280 calories, 19g fat (6g immersed fat), 73mg cholesterol, 519mg sodium, 4g starch (2g sugars, 1g fiber), 23g protein. Diabetic Exchanges: 3 lean meat, 1-1/2 fat, 1 vegetable.

Grilled Salmon with Nectarines

Ingredients

- 4 salmon filets (4 ounces each)
- 1/2 teaspoon salt, iodized
- 1/8 teaspoon pepper
- 1 tablespoon nectar
- 1 tablespoon lemon juice
- 1 tablespoon olive oil
- 3 medium nectarines, sliced

- 1 tablespoon minced fresh basil

Directions

- Sprinkle salmon with 1/4 teaspoon salt and pepper. Spot on an oiled flame broil, skin side down. Flame broil, covered, over medium warmth until fish starts to chips effectively with a fork, 8-10 minutes.
- Then, in a bowl, mix honey, lemon juice, oil and staying salt. Mix in nectarines and basil. Present with salmon.

Nutritional Facts

1 filet with 1/3 cup nectarines: 307 calories, 16g fat (3g saturated fat), 67mg cholesterol, 507mg sodium, 17g starch (13g sugars, 2g fiber), 23g protein. Diabetic Exchanges: 3 lean meat, 1-1/2 fat, 1 fruit.

Tomato-Garlic Lentil Bowls

Fixings

- 1 tablespoon olive oil
- 2 onions, cleaved
- 4 garlic cloves, minced
- 2 cups dried dark-colored lentils, rinsed
- 1 teaspoon salt
- 1/2 teaspoon ground ginger
- 1/2 teaspoon paprika
- 1/4 teaspoon pepper

- 3 cups of water
- 1/4 cup lemon juice
- 3 tablespoons tomato paste
- 3/4 cup without fat plain Greek yogurt
- Optional: Chopped tomatoes and minced fresh cilantro

Directions

- In a large pot, heat oil over medium-high warmth; saute onions for 2 minutes. Add garlic and cook for 1 minute. Mix in lentils, seasonings, and water; heat to the point of boiling. Decrease heat; stew, until lentils are delicate, 25-30 minutes.
- Mix in lemon juice and tomato paste; heat through. Present with yogurt and, whenever wanted, tomatoes and cilantro.
- Health Tip: Cup for the cup, lentils have twice as a lot of protein and iron as quinoa.

Nutritional Facts

3/4 cup: 294 calories, 3g fat (0 immersed fat), 0 cholesterol, 419mg sodium, 49g starch (5g sugars, 8g fiber), 21g protein. Diabetic exchanges: 3 starch, 2 lean meat, 1/2 fat.

Mediterranean Turkey Skillet

Ingredients

- 1 tablespoon olive oil
- 1 bundle (20 ounces) lean ground turkey
- 2 medium zucchini, cut into 1/2 inch cubes
- 1 onion, chopped
- 2 banana peppers, seeded and chopped
- 3 garlic cloves, minced
- 1/2 teaspoon dried oregano
- 1 can (15 ounces) dark beans, washed
- \1 can (14-1/2 ounces) diced tomatoes,

- 1 tablespoon balsamic vinegar
- 1/2 teaspoon salt

Directions

- In a large skillet, heat oil over medium-high warmth. Add turkey, zucchini, onion, peppers, garlic, and oregano; cook 10-12 minutes or until turkey is done and vegetables are delicate, drain.
- Mix in the remaining ingredients; heat through, blending every so often.

Nutrition Facts

1 cup: 259 calories, 10g fat (2g soaked fat), 65mg cholesterol, 504mg sodium, 20g starch (6g sugars, 6g fiber), 24g protein. Diabetic Exchanges: 3 lean meat, 1 vegetable, 1/2 starch, 1/2 fat.

Chicken Thighs with Shallots & Spinach

Ingredients

- 6 boneless skinless chicken thighs
- 1/2 teaspoon salt
- 1/2 teaspoon pepper
- 1-1/2 teaspoons olive oil
- 4 shallots, thinly sliced
- 1/3 cup white wine or low sodium chicken broth

- 1 bundle (10 ounces) spinach, cut
- 1/4 teaspoon salt
- 1/4 cup low fat sharp cream

Directions

- Sprinkle chicken with prepared salt and pepper. In a large nonstick skillet, heat oil over medium warmth. Add chicken; cook until 170°, around 6 minutes on each side. Remove from skillet; keep warm.
- In the same pan, cook and mix shallots until delicate. Add wine; heat to the point of boiling. Cook until wine is reduced significantly. Add spinach and salt; cook and mix just until spinach is wilted. Mix in sharp cream; present with chicken.

Freeze choice: Before adding sour cream, cool chicken and spinach blend. To utilize, mostly defrost in cooler medium-term. Warm through gradually in a skillet, mixing until a thermometer reads 170°. Mix in sharp cream.

Nutrition Facts

1 chicken thigh with 1/4 cup spinach blend: 223 calories, 10g fat (3g soaked fat), 77mg cholesterol, 360mg sodium, 7g starch (2g sugars, 1g fiber), 23g protein. Diabetic Exchanges: 3 lean meat, 1-1/2 fat, 1 vegetable.

Balsamic-Glazed Beef Skewers

Ingredients

- 1/4 cup balsamic vinaigrette
- 1/4 cup barbecue sauce
- 1 teaspoon Dijon mustard
- 1 pound meat top sirloin steak, cut into 1-inch squares
- 2 cups cherry tomatoes

Directions

- In a large bowl, whisk vinaigrette, grill sauce, and mustard until mixed. Save 1/4 cup blend for seasoning. Add beef to outstanding blend; toss to cover.
- Then string meat and tomatoes on four metal or wooden sticks. Barbecue sticks over medium warmth or sear 4 in. from heat 6-9 minutes or until meat arrives at wanted doneness, turning once in a while and treating every now and again withheld vinaigrette blend during the most recent 3 minutes.

Nutritional Facts

1 screw: 194 calories, 7g fat (2g immersed fat), 46mg cholesterol, 288mg sodium, 7g starch (5g sugars, 1g fiber), 25g protein. Diabetic Exchanges: 3 lean meat, 1-1/2 fat, 1/2 starch.

Pronto Vegetarian Peppers

Ingredients

- 2 large sweet red peppers
- 1 cup canned stewed tomatoes
- 1/3 cup dark colored rice
- 2 tablespoons boiling water
- 3/4 cup canned kidney beans, washed
- 1/2 cup corn, thawed
- 2 green onions, thinly sliced

- 1/8 teaspoon squashed red pepper chips
- 1/2 cup destroyed part-skim mozzarella cheese
- 1 tablespoon ground Parmesan cheese

Directions

- Cut peppers down the middle longwise; remove seeds. Peppers in an ungreased shallow microwave-safe dish. Spread and microwave on high until tender, 3-4 minutes.
- Combine the tomatoes, rice, and water in a little microwave-safe bowl. Spread and microwave on high until rice is done, 5-6 minutes. Mix in the beans, corn, onions and pepper chips; spoon into peppers.
- Sprinkle with cheeses. Microwave, uncovered, until warmed through, 3-4 minutes.

Nutrition Facts

2 stuffed pepper parts: 341 calories, 7g fat (3g immersed fat), 19mg cholesterol, 556mg sodium, 56g starch (16g sugars, 11g fiber), and 19g protein.

Mediterranean Chickpeas

Ingredients

- 1 cup water
- 3/4 cup uncooked whole wheat couscous
- 1 tablespoon olive oil
- 1 medium onion, chopped
- 2 garlic cloves, minced
- 1 can (15 ounces) chickpeas or garbanzo beans

- ♦ 1 can (14-1/2 ounces) no-salt-addd stewed tomatoes, cut up
- ♦ 1 can (14 ounces) water-pressed artichoke hearts
- ♦ 1/2 cup pitted Greek olives, coarsely chopped
- ♦ 1 tablespoon lemon juice
- ♦ 1/2 teaspoon dried oregano
- ♦ Dash of pepper
- ♦ Dash of cayenne pepper

Directions

- In a small saucepan, heat water to the point of boiling. Mix in couscous. Remove from heat; let stand, covered, 5-10 minutes or until water is absorbed.
- In the meantime, in a large nonstick skillet, heat oil over medium-high heat. Add onion; cook and mix until delicate. Add garlic; cook brief longer. Sir in residual ingredients; heat through, blending periodically. Present with couscous.

Nutrition Facts

1 cup chickpea blend with 2/3 cup couscous: 340 calories, 10g fat (1g immersed fat), 0 cholesterol, 677mg sodium, 51g starch (9g sugars, 9g fiber), and 11g protein.

Rosemary Chicken with Spinach & Beans

Ingredients

- 1 can (14-1/2 ounces) stewed tomatoes
- 4 boneless skinless chicken bosom parts (6 ounces each)
- 2 teaspoons dried rosemary, crushed
- 1/2 teaspoon salt
- 1/2 teaspoon pepper
- 4 teaspoons olive oil1 bundle (6 ounces) spinach
- 2 garlic cloves, minced
- 1 can (15 ounces) cannellini beans, washed and drained

Directions

- Drain tomatoes, saving juice; coarsely hack tomatoes. Pound chicken with a meat hammer to 1/4-in. thickness. Rub with rosemary, salt, and pepper. In a large skillet, heat 2 teaspoons oil over medium warmth. Add chicken; cook 5-6 minutes on each side. Remove and keep warm.
- In the same pan, heat remaining oil over medium-high heat. Add spinach and garlic; cook and mix 2-3 minutes or until spinach is wilted. Mix in beans, tomatoes and saved juice; heat through. Present with chicken.

Nutrition Facts

1 chicken breast half with 3/4 cup sauce: 348 calories, 9g fat (2g immersed fat), 94mg cholesterol, 729mg sodium, 25g starch (5g sugars, 6g fiber), and 41g protein. Diabetic Exchanges: 5 lean meat, 2 vegetable, 1 starch, and 1 fat.

Skillet Beef and Potatoes

Ingredients

- 1-1/2 pounds red potatoes (around 5 medium), divided and cut into 1/4-inch cuts
- 1/3 cup water
- 1/2 teaspoon salt
- 1 pound beef top sirloin steak, cut into strips
- 1/2 cup sliced onion
- 3 tablespoons olive oil
- 2 teaspoons garlic pepper mix
- 1-1/2 teaspoons minced rosemary

Directions

- Potatoes, water, and salt in a microwave-safe dish; microwave on high until potatoes are tender, 7-9 minutes. Drain.
- In the meantime, toss beef with onion, 2 tablespoons oil and pepper mix. A large skillet over medium-high warmth. Add half of the meat blend; cook and mix until hamburger is browned, 1-2 minutes. Remove from dish; rehash with outstanding beef mixture.
- In a skillet, heat remaining oil over medium-high warmth. Add potatoes; cook until gently sautéed, 4-5 minutes, turning at times. Mix in beef mixture; heat through. Sprinkle with rosemary.

Nutrition Facts

1-1 /2 cups: 320 calories, 16g fat (4g soaked fat), 63mg cholesterol, 487mg sodium, 20g starch (2g sugars, 2g fiber), and 23g protein. Diabetic Exchanges: 3 lean meat, 2 fat, 1 starch.

Lemon-Lime Salmon with Veggie Saute

Ingredients

- 6 salmon filets (4 ounces each)
- 1/2 cup lemon juice
- 1/2 cup lime juice
- 1 teaspoon seafood flavoring

- 1/4 teaspoon salt
- 2 medium sweet red peppers, cut
- 2 medium sweet yellow peppers, cut
- 1 large red onion, divided and cut
- 2 teaspoons olive oil
- 1 bundle (10 ounces) frozen corn, defrosted
- 2 cups child portobello mushrooms
- 2 cups cut fresh asparagus (1-inch pieces)
- 2 tablespoons minced fresh tarragon or 2 teaspoons dried tarragon

Directions

- Place salmon in a 13x9-in. baking dish; Add lemon and lime juices. Sprinkle with fish flavoring and salt. Heat, uncovered, at 425° until fish flakes effectively with a fork, 10-15 minutes.
- Then, in a skillet coated with cooking spray, saute peppers and onion in for 3 minutes. Add the corn, mushrooms, and asparagus; cook and mix just until vegetables arrive at wanted doneness, 3-4 minutes longer. Mix in tarragon. Present with salmon.

Nutritional Facts

1 filet with 1-1/4 cups vegetables: 329 calories, 15g fat (3g immersed fat), 67mg cholesterol, 283mg sodium, 25g starch (7g sugars, 4g fiber), and 27g protein.

Diabetic Exchanges: 3 lean meat, 1-1/2 starch, 1-1/2 fat.

Tuscan Chicken and Beans

Ingredients

- 1 pound boneless skinless chicken bosoms, cut into 3/4-inch cubes
- 2 teaspoons minced fresh rosemary or 1/2 teaspoon dried rosemary
- 1/4 teaspoon salt
- 1/4 teaspoon ground pepper
- 1 cup reduced sodium chicken broth
- 2 tablespoons sun-dried tomatoes (not stuffed in oil), chopped

- 1 can (15-1/2 ounces) cannellini beans

Directions

- In a little bowl, combine the chicken, rosemary, salt and pepper. In a large nonstick skillet covered with splash guard, cook chicken over medium heat until browned.
- Mix in broth and tomatoes. Heat to the point of boiling. Reduce heat; stew, uncovered, for 3-5 minutes or until chicken juices run clear. Add beans; heat through.

Nutritional Facts

1 cup: 216 calories, 3g fat (1g immersed fat), 63mg cholesterol, 517mg sodium, 17g starch (1g sugars, 4g fiber), 28g protein. Diabetic Exchanges: 3 lean meat, 1 starch.

Mediterranean Tilapia

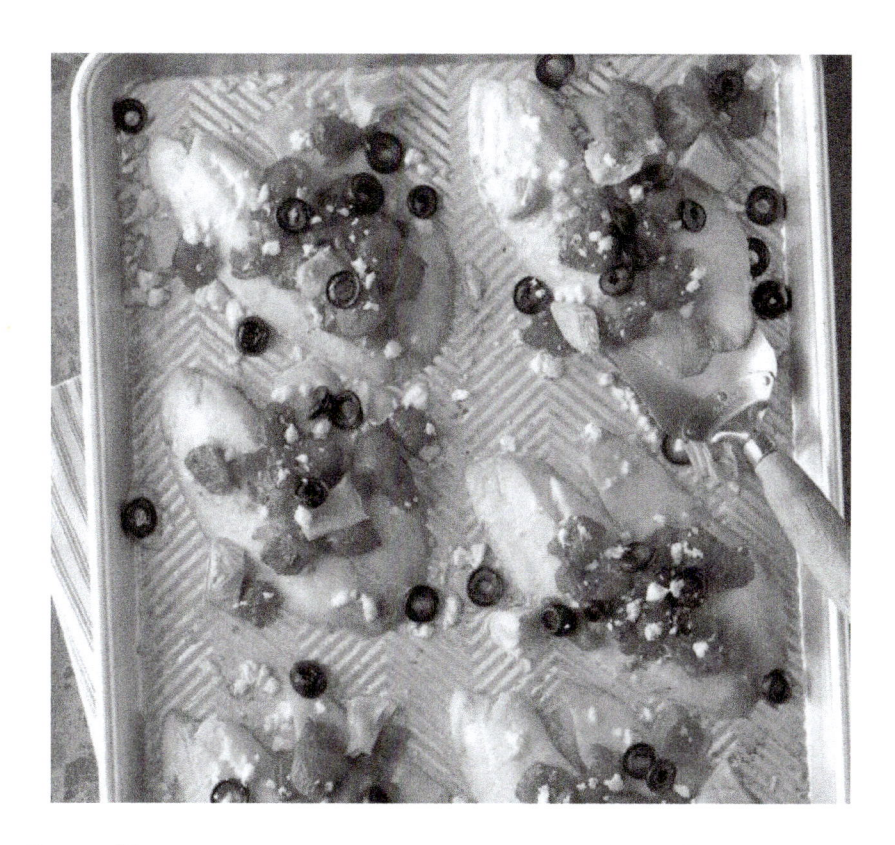

Ingredients:

- 6 tilapia filets (6 ounces each)
- 1 cup canned Italian diced tomatoes
- 1/2 cup water-pressed artichoke hearts1/2 cup cut ready olives
- 1/2 cup crumbled feta cheese

Directions

- Preheat broiler to 400°. Filets in a 15x10x1-in. skillet coated with cooking spray. Top with tomatoes, artichoke hearts, olives, and feta. Prepare, uncovered, until fish chips effectively with a fork, 15-20 minutes.

Italian Tilapia: Follow method as coordinated yet top filets with 1 cup diced tomatoes with simmered garlic, 1/2 cup each julienned cooked sweet red pepper, cut mushrooms and diced crisp mozzarella cheese, and 1/2 tsp. dried basil. **1 filet:** 189 calories, 4 g fat (2 g soaked fat), 90 mg cholesterol, 351 mg sodium, 4 g starch, 2 g fiber, 34 g protein. **Diabetic exchanges:** 5 lean meat, 1/2 fat.

Southwest Tilapia: Follow method as intructed yet top filets with 1 cup diced tomatoes with mild green chiles, 1/2 cup cubed avocado, corn (defrosted) and cubed feta, and 1/2 tsp. dried cilantro.

1 filet: 224 calories, 7 g fat (3 g soaked fat), 93 mg cholesterol, 281 mg sodium, 7 g sugar, 2 g fiber, 35 g protein. **Diabetic exchanges:** 5 lean meat, 1 fat.

Nutrition Facts

1 filet: 197 calories, 4g fat (2g soaked fat), 88mg cholesterol, 446mg sodium, 5g starch (2g sugars, 1g fiber), 34g protein. Diabetic exchanges: 5 lean meat, 1/2 fat.

California Quinoa

Ingredients

- 1 tablespoon olive oil
- 1 cup quinoa
- 2 garlic cloves, minced
- 1 medium zucchini, sliced
- 2 cups water
- 3/4 cup canned garbanzo beans or chickpeas

- 1 medium tomato, finely chopped
- 1/2 cup shredded feta
- 1/4 cup finely chopped Greek olives
- 2 tablespoons minced fresh basil
- 1/4 teaspoon pepper

Directions

- In a large saucepan, heat oil over medium-high warmth. Add quinoa and garlic; cook and mix 2-3 minutes or until quinoa is gently seared. Mix in zucchini and water; heat to the point of boiling. Reduce heat; stew, covered, 12-15 minutes. Mix in remaining ingredients; heat through.

Nutrition Facts

1 cup: 310 calories, 11g fat (3g soaked fat), 8mg cholesterol, 353mg sodium, 42g starch (3g sugars, 6g fiber), 11g protein. Diabetic Exchanges: 2 starch, 1-1/2 fat, 1 lean meat, 1 vegetable.

Salmon with Root Vegetables

Ingredients

- 2 tablespoons olive oil
- 2 sweet potatoes, peeled and cut into 1/4-inch cubes
- 2 red potatoes, cut into 1/4-inch cubes
- 2 turnips, peeled and diced
- 2 carrots, peeled and diced
- 1 teaspoon sea salt1 teaspoon chili powder

- 3/4 teaspoon pepper
- 1/2 teaspoon ground cinnamon
- 1/2 teaspoon ground cumin
- 6 salmon filets (6 ounces each)

Directions

- Preheat oven to 400°. In a large skillet, heat oil over medium heat. Add potatoes, turnips, and carrots. Combine 1/2 teaspoon salt, bean stew powder, 1/2 teaspoon pepper, cinnamon, and cumin; sprinkle over vegetables. Cook, mixing often, until vegetables are tender, 15-20 minutes.
- Place salmon, skin side down, in a foil-lined 15x10x1-in. baking pan. Sprinkle with staying salt and pepper. Oven; sear until fish just starts to drop effectively, 2-5 minutes. Serve salmon with vegetables.

Test Kitchen Tips

Settle a poached egg in the vegetables, and get a 6g increase in protein. Roasting draws out the characteristic sweetness of root vegetables, ideal for getting kids (and numerous grown-ups) to eat them.

Nutrition Facts

1 serving: 417 calories, 21g fat (4g immersed fat), 85mg cholesterol, 464mg sodium, 26g starch (9g sugars, 4g fiber), 31g protein. Diabetic trades: 4 lean meat, 2 starch, and 1 fat.

Mediterranean Chicken Stir-Fry

Ingredients

- 2 cups water
- 1 cup quick cooking grain
- 1 pound boneless skinless chicken bosoms, cubed
- 3 teaspoons olive oil
- 1 medium onion, chopped
- 2 medium zucchini, chopped
- 2 garlic cloves, minced
- 1 teaspoon dried oregano

- 1/2 teaspoon dried basil
- 1/4 teaspoon salt
- 1/4 teaspoon pepper
- Dash squashed red pepper chips
- 2 plum tomatoes, chopped
- 1/2 cup set Greek olives, chopped
- 1 tablespoon minced parsley

Directions

- In a little saucepan, heat water to the point of boiling. Mix in barley. Reduce heat; spread and stew for 10-12 minutes or until grain is tender. Remove from the heat; let sit for 5 minutes.
- In the meantime, in a large skillet or wok, pan sear chicken in 2 teaspoons oil until never again pink. Remove and keep warm.
- Stir-fry onion in remaining oil for 3 minutes. Add the zucchini, garlic, oregano, basil, salt, pepper and pepper pieces; pan sear 2-4 minutes longer or until vegetables are fresh tender. Add the chicken, tomatoes, olives, and parsley. Present with barley.

Nutrition Facts

1 cup chicken mixture with 3/4 cup grain: 403 calories, 12g fat (2g soaked fat), 63mg cholesterol, 498mg sodium, 44g starch (5g sugars, 11g fiber), 31g protein. Diabetic Exchanges: 3 lean meat, 2 starch, 2 fat, 1 vegetable.

Stuffed-Olive Cod

Ingredients

- 4 cod filets (6 ounces each)
- 1 teaspoon dried oregano
- 1/4 teaspoon salt
- 1 medium lemon,
- 1 shallot, thinly cut
- 1/3 cup garlic-stuffed olives, cut in half
- 2 tablespoons water
- 2 tablespoons olive juice

Directions

- Filets in a large nonstick skillet covered with cooking spray. Sprinkle with oregano and salt; top with lemon and shallot.
- Spread olives around fish; add water and olive juice. Heat to the point of boiling. Reduce warmth to low; delicately cook, covered, 8-10 minutes or until fish just starts to flake with a fork.

Nutrition Facts

1 filet: 163 calories, 3g fat (0 saturated fat), 65mg cholesterol, 598mg sodium, 4g starch (1g sugars, 0 fiber), 27g protein. Diabetic Exchanges: 4 lean meat.

Tuna and White Bean Lettuce Wraps

Ingredients

- 1 can (12 ounces) light tuna in water
- 1 can (15 ounces) cannellini beans
- 1/4 cup chopped red onion
- 2 tablespoons olive oil
- 1 tablespoon minced fresh parsley

- 1/8 teaspoon salt
- 1/8 teaspoon pepper
- 12 Bibb or Boston lettuce leaves (around 1 medium head)
- 1 medium ripe avocado, peeled and cut

Directions

- In a little bowl, combine the initial 7 ingredients; toss delicately to combine. Serve in lettuce leaves; top with avocado.

Nutrition Facts

3 wraps: 279 calories, 13g fat (2g immersed fat), 31mg cholesterol, 421mg sodium, 19g starch (1g sugars, 7g fiber), 22g protein. Diabetic Exchanges: 3 lean meat, 2 fat, 1 starch.

Whole Wheat Orzo Salad

Ingredients

- 2-1/2 cups uncooked whole wheat orzo pasta (around 1 pound)
- 1 can (15 ounces) cannellini beans
- 3 tomatoes, finely chopped
- 1 English cucumber, finely chopped
- 2 cups crumbled feta cheese

- 1-1/4 cups set Greek olives (around 6 ounces), chopped
- 1 sweet yellow pepper, finely chopped
- 1 green pepper, finely chopped
- 1 cup mint leaves, chopped
- 1/2 red onion, finely sliced
- 1/4 cup lemon juice
- 2 tablespoons olive oil
- 1 lemon zest
- 3 garlic cloves, minced
- 1/2 teaspoon pepper

Directions

- Cook orzo as indicated by package directions. Drain orzo; wash with cold water.
- In the meantime, in a large bowl, join remaining ingredients. Mix in orzo. Refrigerate until serving.

Nutritional Facts

1-3/4 cups: 411 calories, 17g fat (4g immersed fat), 15mg cholesterol, 740mg sodium, 51g starch (3g sugars, 13g fiber), and 14g protein.

Garden Quinoa Salad

Ingredients

- 1-1/2 cups quinoa, washed and drained
- 3 cups water
- 1 pound fresh asparagus, cut into 2-inch pieces
- 1/2 pound fresh sugar snap peas
- 1/2 pound fresh green beans, trimmed
- 2 tablespoons olive oil
- 2 tablespoons lemon juice
- 2 tablespoons minced fresh parsley

- 1 teaspoon ground lemon
- 3/4 teaspoon salt
- 1 cup cherry tomatoes, halved
- 3 tablespoons salted pumpkin seeds or pepitas

Directions

- In a large saucepan, cook and mix quinoa over medium-high warmth 3-5 minutes or until toasted. Add water; heat to the point of boiling. Decrease heat; stew, covered, 12-15 minutes. Move to a large bowl.
- In the meantime, in an large pan, heat 4 cups water to the point of boiling. Add asparagus and snap peas; cook, uncovered, 2-4 minutes. Remove vegetables and promptly drop into ice water.
- Return water to a boil. Add green beans; cook 3-4 minutes. Remove beans and drop into ice water, vegetables; pat dry.
- In a small bowl, whisk oil, lemon juice, parsley, lemon zest and salt. Add tomatoes and vegetables to quinoa; shower with dressing and toss to combine. Top with pumpkin seeds.

Nutrition Facts

2-1/4 cups with around 2 teaspoons pumpkin seeds: 417 calories, 15g fat (2g saturated fat), 0 cholesterol, 533mg sodium, 58g starch (6g sugars, 9g fiber), and 16g protein.

Mahi Mahi & Veggie Skillet

Ingredients

- 3 tablespoons olive oil
- 4 mahi or salmon filets (6 ounces each)
- 3 sweet red peppers, cut into thick strips
- 1/2 pound sliced portobello mushrooms
- 1 large sweet onion, cut into thick rings and isolated
- 1/3 cup lemon juice

- 3/4 teaspoon salt
- 1/2 teaspoon pepper
- 1/4 cup minced fresh chives
- 1/3 cup pine nuts, optional

Directions

- In a large skillet, heat 2 tablespoons oil over medium-high warmth. Add filets; cook 4-5 minutes on each side or until fish just starts to break with a fork. Remove from pan.
- Add remaining oil, peppers, mushrooms, onion, lemon juice and 1/4 teaspoon salt. Cook, covered, over medium warmth until vegetables are delicate, blending at times, 6-8 minutes.
- Place fish over vegetables; sprinkle with pepper and remaining salt. Cook, covered, 2 minutes longer or until warmed through. Sprinkle with chives and, whenever wanted, pine nuts before serving.

Nutrition Facts

1 serving: 307 calories, 12g fat (2g soaked fat), 124mg cholesterol, 606mg sodium, 15g starch (9g sugars, 3g fiber), 35g protein. Diabetic Exchanges: 4 lean meat, 3 vegetable, 2 fat.

Lemon-Olive Chicken with Orzo

Ingredients

- 1 tablespoon olive oil
- 4 boneless skinless chicken thighs (around 1 pound)
- 1 can (14-1/2 ounces) reduced sodium chicken broth
- 2/3 cup uncooked whole wheat orzo pasta
- 1/2 lemon, cut into 4 wedges
- 1/2 cup set Greek olives, sliced

- 1 tablespoon lemon juice
- 1 teaspoon dried oregano
- 1/4 teaspoon pepper

Directions

- In a large nonstick skillet, heat oil over medium warmth. Sear chicken on the two sides; remove from skillet.
- Add broth to skillet; increase warmth to medium-high. Cook 1-2 minutes, mixing to slacken caramelized bits from skillet. Mix in remaining ingredients; heat to the point of boiling. Decrease heat; stew, uncovered, 5 minutes, mixing often.
- Return chicken to dish. Cook, covered, 5-8 minutes or until pasta is delicate and a thermometer embedded in chicken read 170°.

Nourishment Facts

1 serving: 345 calories, 17g fat (3g soaked fat), 76mg cholesterol, 636mg sodium, 22g starch (1g sugars, 5g fiber), 26g protein. Diabetic Exchanges: 3 lean meat, 2 fat, 1 starch.

Blackened Tilapia with Zucchini Noodles

Ingredients

- 2 large zucchini (around 1-1/2 pounds)
- 1-1/2 teaspoons ground cumin
- 3/4 teaspoon salt, separated
- 1/2 teaspoon smoked paprika
- 1/2 teaspoon pepper
- 1/4 tsp garlic powder
- 4 tilapia filets (6 ounces each)

- 2 teaspoons olive oil
- 2 garlic cloves, minced
- 1 cup pico de gallo

Directions

- Trim parts of the zucchini. Utilizing a spiralizer, cut zucchini into dainty strands.
- Mix cumin, 1/2 teaspoon salt, smoked paprika, pepper and garlic powder; sprinkle liberally onto the two sides of tilapia. In a large nonstick skillet, heat oil over medium-high warmth. In batches, cook tilapia until fish just starts to break with a fork, 2-3 minutes for each side. Remove from skillet; keep warm.
- In same pan, cook zucchini with garlic over medium-high warmth until somewhat relaxed, 1-2 minutes, tossing always with tongs (don't overcook). Sprinkle with salt. Present with tilapia and pico de gallo.

Nutrition Facts

1 serving: 203 calories, 4g fat (1g saturated fat), 83mg cholesterol, 522mg sodium, 8g starch (5g sugars, 2g fiber), 34g protein. Diabetic Exchanges: 5 lean meat, 1 vegetable, 1/2 fat.

Sweet-Chili Salmon with Blackberries

Ingredients

- 1 cup crisp lackberries,
- 1 cup finely chopped English cucumber
- 1 green onion, finely sliced
- 2 tablespoons sweet chili sauce
- 4 salmon filets (6 ounces each)
- 1/2 teaspoon salt
- 1/2 teaspoon pepper

Directions

- In a little bowl, join blackberries, cucumber, green onion and 1 tablespoon chili sauce; toss to cover. Sprinkle salmon with salt and pepper.
- Spot filets on greased grill rack, skin side down. Flame broil, covered, over medium-high warmth or cook 4 in. from heat 10-12 minutes or until fish pieces effectively with a fork, brushing with residual bean stew sauce during the last 2-3 minutes of cooking. Present with blackberry mixture.

Nutritional Facts

1 filet with 1/2 cup berry blend: 303 calories, 16g fat (3g immersed fat), 85mg cholesterol,

510mg sodium, 9g starch (6g sugars, 2g fiber), 30g protein. Diabetic Exchanges: 5 lean meat, 1/2 starch.

Arugula & Brown Rice Salad

Ingredients

- 1 bundle (8.8 ounces) prepared to-serve brown rice
- 7 cups crisp arugula or baby spinach (around 5 ounces)
- 1 can (15 ounces) garbanzo beans or chickpeas, rinsed and drained
- 1 cup (4 ounces) disintegrated feta cheese
- 3/4 cup inexactly pressed basil leaves, torn
- 1/2 cup dried fruits or cranberries
- DRESSING:

- 1/4 cup olive oil
- 1/4 teaspoon ground lemon zest
- 2 tablespoons lemon juice
- 1/4 teaspoon salt
- 1/8 teaspoon pepper

Directions

- Warmth rice. Move to an large bowl; cool marginally.
- Mix arugula, beans, cheese, basil and fruits into rice. In a little bowl, whisk dressing ingredients. Sprinkle over serving of mixed greens; toss to cover. Serve right away.

Nutrition Facts

2 cups: 473 calories, 22g fat (5g immersed fat), 15mg cholesterol, 574mg sodium, 53g starch (17g sugars, 7g fiber), 13g protein.

Sauteed Pork Chops with Garlic Spinach

Ingredients

- 1 tablespoon olive oil
- 4 bone-in pork loin chops (8 ounces each)
- 1/4 teaspoon salt
- 1/4 teaspoon pepper
- 1 lemon

GARLIC SPINACH:

- 1 tablespoon olive oil
- 3 garlic cloves, meagerly cut
- 2 bundles (5 ounces each) crisp spinach, stems removeled
- 1/2 teaspoon salt
- 1/4 teaspoon ground pepper
- 1 teaspoon lemon juice

Directions

- In a large skillet, heat oil over medium-high warmth. Sprinkle pork cleaves with salt and pepper; add to skillet. Saute until a thermometer peruses 145°, around 5 minutes for every side. Evacuate to a serving platter; squeeze juice from lemon over chops. Tent with foil; let remain at least 5 minutes before serving.
- For garlic spinach, heat oil over medium-high warmth in same skillet. Add garlic; cook until it just starts to darker, around 45 seconds. Add spinach; cook and mix just until shriveled, 2-3 minutes. Sprinkle with salt and pepper. Remove from heat; add lemon juice. Move to serving platter. Remove foil from pork; serve spinach with chops.

Nutrition Facts

1 Pork hack with 1/2 cup spinach: 310 calories, 17g fat (5g soaked fat), 98mg cholesterol, 607mg sodium, 4g starch (1g sugars, 1g fiber), 36g protein. Diabetic Exchanges: 4 lean meat, 1-1/2 fat, 1 vegetable.

Warm Rice & Pintos Salad

Fixings

- 1 tablespoon olive oil
- 1 cup solidified corn
- 1 little onion, cut
- 2 garlic cloves, minced
- 1-1/2 teaspoons chili powder
- 1-1/2 teaspoons ground cumin
- 1 can (15 ounces) pinto beans, washed

- 1 bundle (8.8 ounces) prepared to-serve dark colored rice
- 1 can (4 ounces) chopped green chilies
- 1/2 cup salsa
- 1/4 cup chopped crisp cilantro
- 1 pack romaine, quartered the long way through the core
- 1/4 cup finely shredded cheese

Directions

- In a large skillet, heat oil over medium-high warmth. Add corn and onion; cook and mix 4-5 minutes or until onion is tender. Mix in garlic, bean stew powder and cumin; cook and mix brief longer.
- Add beans, rice, green chilies, salsa and cilantro; heat through, mixing once in a while.
- Serve over romaine wedges. Sprinkle with cheese.

Nutrition Facts

1 serving: 331 calories, 8g fat (2g soaked fat), 7mg cholesterol, 465mg sodium, 50g starch (5g sugars, 9g fiber), 12g protein. Diabetic Exchanges: 2-1/2 starch, 2 vegetable, 1 lean meat, 1/2 fat.

Chicken & Goat Cheese Skillet

Ingredients

- 1/2 pound boneless skinless chicken breasts, cut into 1-inch pieces
- 1/4 teaspoon salt
- 1/8 teaspoon pepper
- 2 teaspoons olive oil
- 1 cup cut crisp asparagus (1-inch pieces)
- 1 garlic clove, minced

- 3 plum tomatoes, chopped
- 3 tablespoons 2% milk
- 2 tablespoons herbed fresh goat cheese, crumbled. Hot cooked rice or pasta
- Extra goat cheese, optional

Directions

- Toss chicken with salt and pepper. In a large skillet, heat oil over medium-high warmth; saute chicken 4-6 minutes. Remove from skillet; keep warm.
- Add asparagus to skillet; cook and mix over medium-high warmth 1 moment. Add garlic; cook and mix 30 seconds. Mix in tomatoes, milk and 2 tablespoons cheese; cook, covered, over medium warmth until cheese starts to soften, 2-3 minutes. Mix in chicken. Present with rice. Whenever wanted, top with extra cheese.

Nutrition Facts

1-1 /2 cups chicken blend: 251 calories, 11g fat (3g soaked fat), 74mg cholesterol, 447mg sodium, 8g starch (5g sugars, 3g fiber), and 29g protein. Diabetic Exchanges: 4 lean meat, 2 fat, 1 vegetable.

Lemon Salmon with Basil

Ingredients

- 4 salmon filets (6 ounces each)
- 2 teaspoons olive oil
- 1 lemon zest
- 1/2 teaspoon salt
- 1/4 teaspoon pepper
- 2 tablespoons cut basil
- 2 lemons, cut
- Additional fresh basil

Directions

- Preheat ovento 375°. Salmon in a lubed 15x10x1-in. heating dish. Shower with oil; sprinkle with lemon zest, salt, pepper and 2 tablespoons basil; top with lemon cuts.
- Prepare 15-20 minutes or until fish just starts to piece until it flakes with a fork. Whenever wanted, top with extra basil.

Nutrition Facts

1 salmon filet: 294 calories, 18g fat (3g soaked fat), 85mg cholesterol, 381mg sodium, 3g starch (1g sugars, 1g fiber), 29g protein. Diabetic Exchanges: 5 lean meat, 1/2 fat.

Greek Fish Bake

Ingredients

- 4 cod filets (6 ounces each)
- 2 tablespoons olive oil
- 1/4 teaspoon salt
- 1/8 teaspoon pepper
- 1 green pepper, cut into thin strips
- 1/2 red onion, daintily cut
- 1/4 cup set Greek olives, sliced

- 1 can (8 ounces) tomato sauce
- 1/4 cup crumbled feta cheese

Directions

- Preheat oven to 400°. Cod in a lubed 13x9-in. preparing dish. Brush with oil; sprinkle with salt and pepper. Top with green pepper, onion and olives.
- Pour tomato sauce over top; sprinkle with cheese. Prepare until fish just starts to break with a fork, 15-20 minutes.

Nutrition Facts

1 filet with garnishes: 246 calories, 12g fat (2g immersed fat), 68mg cholesterol, 706mg sodium, 6g starch (2g sugars, 2g fiber), 29g protein. Diabetic Exchanges: 4 lean meat, 1-1/2 fat, 1 vegetable.

Caesar Salmon with Roasted Tomatoes & Artichokes

Ingredients

- 4 salmon filets (5 ounces each)
- 5 tablespoons reduceed fat Caesar vinaigrette, separated
- 1/4 teaspoon pepper
- 2 cups grape tomatoes
- 1 can (14 ounces) water-pressed artichoke hearts

- 1 sweet orange or yellow pepper, cut into 1-inch pieces

Directions

- Preheat broiler to 425°. Spot salmon on half of a 15x10x1-in. heating container covered with cooking splash. Brush with 2 tablespoons vinaigrette; sprinkle with 1/8 teaspoon pepper.
- In a large bowl, join tomatoes, artichoke hearts and sweet pepper. Add the rest of the vinaigrette and pepper; toss to cover. Spot tomato blend on staying half of container. Broil until fish just starts to piece effectively with a fork and vegetables are delicate, 12-15 minutes.

Nutrition Facts

1 filet with 3/4 cup tomato blend: 318 calories, 16g fat (3g soaked fat), 73mg cholesterol, 674mg sodium, 12g starch (4g sugars, 2g fiber), 28g protein. Diabetic Exchanges: 4 lean meat, 1 vegetable, 1 fat.

Citrus Scallops

Ingredients

- 1 medium green or sweet red pepper, julienned
- 4 green onions, chopped
- 1 garlic clove, minced
- 2 tablespoons olive oil
- 1 pound ocean scallops
- 1/2 teaspoon salt
- 1/4 teaspoon squashed red pepper pieces
- 2 tablespoons lime juice
- 1/2 teaspoon grated lime zest

- 4 medium navel oranges, peeled and segmented
- 2 teaspoons minced fresh cilantro
- Hot cooked rice or pasta

Directions

- In a large skillet, saute the pepper, onions, and garlic in oil for 1 minute. Add scallops, salt, and pepper drops; cook for 4 minutes. Add lime squeeze and zest; cook for 1 minute. Decrease heat. Add orange segments and cilantro; cook 2 minutes longer or until scallops are opaque. Present with rice or pasta.

Nutrition Facts

1 serving (determined without rice or pasta): 240 calories, 8g fat (1g soaked fat), 37mg cholesterol, 482mg sodium, 23g starch (14g sugars, 4g fiber), and 21g protein. **Diabetic Exchanges**: 3 lean meat, 1-1/2 fat, and 1 natural product.

Quinoa-Stuffed Squash Boats

Ingredients

- 4 squash (around 12 ounces each)
- 3 teaspoons olive oil
- 1/8 teaspoon pepper
- 1 teaspoon salt
- 1-1/2 cups vegetable stock
- 1 cup quinoa, rinsed
- 1 can (15 ounces) garbanzo beans or chickpeas
- 1/4 cup dried cranberries
- 1 green onion, cut

- 1 teaspoon minced sage
- 1/2 teaspoon ground lemon zest
- 1 teaspoon lemon juice
- 1/2 cup crumbled goat cheese
- 1/4 cup salted pumpkin seeds or pepitas, toasted

Directions

- Preheat oven to 450°. Cut each squash longwise down the middle; evacuate and dispose of seeds. Delicately brush cut sides with 1 teaspoon oil; sprinkle with pepper and 1/2 teaspoon salt. Spot on a heating sheet, chop side down. Heat until delicate, 15-20 minutes.
- In the meantime, in a large pan, combine soup and quinoa; heat to the point of boiling. Lessen heat; stew, covered, until fluid is assimilated, 12-15 minutes.
- Mix in garbanzo beans, cranberries, green onion, sage, lemon juice and the rest of the oil and salt; spoon into squash. Sprinkle with cheese and pumpkin seeds.

Nutrition Facts

1 stuffed squash half: 275 calories, 8g fat (2g immersed fat), 9mg cholesterol, 591mg sodium

, 46g starch (9g sugars, 10g fiber), 9g protein. Diabetic Exchanges: 3 starch, 1 lean meat, 1/2 fat.

Grapefruit-Gremolata Salmon

Ingredients

- 2 medium grapefruit
- 1/4 cup minced parsley
- 1 garlic clove, minced
- 1 tablespoon in addition to 1 teaspoon brown sugar
- 4 salmon filets (6 ounces each)
- 1 tablespoon cumin seeds, squashed
- 1/2 teaspoon salt

- 1/2 teaspoon ground pepper

Directions

- Preheat broiler. Finely grind enough strip from grapefruit to quantify 2 tablespoons. In a little bowl, blend parsley, garlic and grapefruit strip.
- Cut a thin cut from the top and base of every grapefruit; stand grapefruit upstanding on a cutting board. With a blade, cut off strip and external layer from grapefruit. Cut along the layer of each section to remove organic product. Organize areas in a solitary layer on one portion of a foil-lined 15x10x1-in. baking pan. Sprinkle with 1 tablespoon dark brown sugar.
- Salmon on staying half of skillet. Mix cumin seeds, salt, pepper and brown sugar; sprinkle over salmon.
- Cook 3-4 in. from heat 8-10 minutes or until fish just starts to break with a fork and grapefruit is daintily seared. Sprinkle salmon with parsley blend; present with grapefruit.

Nutrition Facts

1 serving: 332 calories, 16g fat (3g soaked fat), 85mg cholesterol, 387mg sodium, 16g starch (13g sugars, 2g fiber), 30g protein. Diabetic Exchanges: 4 lean meat, 1 starch.

Cod with Bacon & Balsamic Tomatoes

Ingredients

- 4 focus cut bacon strips
- 4 cod filets (5 ounces each)
- 1/2 teaspoon salt
- 1/4 teaspoon pepper
- 2 cups grape tomatoes, halved
- 2 tablespoons balsamic vinegar

Directions

- In a large skillet, cook bacon over medium warmth until fresh, mixing once in a while. Remove with an opened spoon; channel on paper towels.
- Sprinkle filets with salt and pepper. Add filets to bacon drippings; cook over medium-high warmth until fish just starts to chip effectively with a fork, 4-6 minutes on each side. Remove and keep warm.
- Add tomatoes to skillet; cook and mix 2-4 minutes. Mix in vinegar; lessen warmth to medium-low. Cook until sauce is thickened, 1-2 minutes longer. Serve cod with tomato mixture and bacon.

Nutrition Facts

1 filet with 1/4 cup tomato blend and 1 tablespoon bacon: 178 calories, 6g fat (2g immersed fat), 64mg cholesterol, 485mg sodium, 5g starch (4g sugars, 1g fiber), 26g protein. Diabetic Exchanges: 4 lean meat, 1 vegetable.

Pizzaiola Chops

Ingredients

- 2 tablespoons olive oil
- 4 boneless pork flank hacks (6 ounces each)
- 1 teaspoon salt
- 1/4 teaspoon pepper
- 2 cups cut portobello mushrooms
- 1 sweet yellow pepper, coarsely chopped
- 1 sweet red pepper, coarsely chopped

- large 4 tomatoes, chopped
- 1/2 cup white wine dry or chicken soup
- 1 tablespoon minced fresh oregano or 1/2 teaspoon dried oregano 2 garlic cloves, minced
- Hot cooked rice, discretionary

Directions

- In a large skillet, heat 1 tablespoon oil over medium-high warmth. Season pork slashes with 1/2 teaspoon salt and 1/8 teaspoon pepper. Darker slashes on the two sides. Remove from container.
- In same container, heat remaining oil over medium-high warmth. Add mushrooms, yellow pepper and red pepper; cook and mix until mushrooms are delicate, 3-4 minutes. Add tomatoes, wine, oregano, garlic and the staying salt and pepper. Heat to the point of boiling. Reduce heat; stew, uncovered, 2 minutes.
- Return chops to pan. Cook, covered, until a thermometer embedded in pork peruses 145°, 5-7 minutes. Let stand 5 minutes. Whenever wanted, present with rice.

Nutrition Facts

1 pork hack and 1 cup vegetable mixture (determined without rice): 351 calories, 17g fat (5g soaked fat), 82mg cholesterol, 647mg sodium, 10g starch (4g sugars, 2g fiber), and 35g protein. Diabetic Exchanges: 5 lean meat, 1-1/2 fat, 1 vegetable.

Garlic Tilapia with Spicy Kale

Ingredients

- 3 tablespoons olive oil, partitioned
- 2 garlic cloves, minced
- 1 teaspoon fennel seed
- 1/2 teaspoon squashed red pepper drops
- 1 bundle kale, cut (around 16 cups)
- 2/3 cup water
- 4 tilapia filets (6 ounces each)
- 3/4 teaspoon pepper

- 1/2 teaspoon garlic salt
- 1 can (15 ounces) cannellini beans
- 1/2 teaspoon salt

Directions

- In a 6-qt. stockpot, heat 1 tablespoon oil over medium warmth. Add garlic, fennel and pepper pieces; cook and mix 1 moment. Add kale and water; heat to the point of boiling. Decrease heat; stew, covered, 10-12 minutes or until kale is delicate.
- Then, sprinkle tilapia with 1/2 teaspoon pepper and garlic salt. In a large skillet, heat remaining oil over medium warmth. Add tilapia; cook 3-4 minutes on each side or until fish just starts to piece effectively with a fork.
- Add beans, salt and remaining pepper to kale; heat through, mixing every so often. Present with tilapia.

Health Tip: Almost 50% of Americans don't get enough nutrient A. One serving gives you multiple times the everyday proposal for this immune-boosting vitamin.

Nutrition Facts

1 filet with 1 cup kale blend: 359 calories, 13g fat (2g immersed fat), 83mg cholesterol, 645mg sodium, 24g starch (0 sugars, 6g fiber), 39g protein. Diabetic Exchanges: 5 lean meat, 2 fat, 1-1/2 starch.

Pepper and Salsa Cod

Ingredients

- 2 cod or haddock filets (6 ounces each)
- 1 teaspoon olive oil
- 1/4 teaspoon salt
- Dash pepper
- 1/3 cup squeezed orange
- 1/4 cup salsa
- 1/3 cup julienned green pepper
- 1/3 cup julienned sweet red pepper

- Hot cooked rice

Directions

- Preheat oven to 350°. Brush the two sides of filets with oil; place in a lubed 11x7-in. preparing dish. Sprinkle with salt and pepper. Pour orange juice over fish; top with salsa and peppers.
- Heat, covered, until fish just starts to piece effectively with a fork, 17-20 minutes. Present with rice.

Nutrition Facts

1 serving: 183 calories, 3g fat (1g immersed fat), 65mg cholesterol, 512mg sodium, 9g starch (6g sugars, 1g fiber), 27g protein. **Diabetic Exchanges:** 4 lean meat, 1 vegetable, 1/2 fat.

Peppered Tuna Kabobs

Ingredients

- 1/2 cup corn, defrosted
- 4 green onions, chopped
- 1 jalapeno pepper, seeded and chopped
- 2 tablespoons coarsely chopped fresh parsley
- 2 tablespoons lime juice
- 1 pound fish steaks, cut into 1-inch cubes
- 1 teaspoon coarsely ground pepper
- 2 large sweet red peppers, cut into 2x1-inch pieces

- ♦ 1 mango, peeled and cut into 1-inch solid shapes

Directions

- For salsa, in a little bowl, join the initial five ingredients; put in a safe spot.
- Rub tuna with pepper. On four metal or drenched wooden sticks, on the other hand string red peppers, fish and mango.
- Sticks on lubed flame broil rack. Cook, covered, over medium warmth, turning once in a while, 10-12 minutes. Present with salsa.

Nourishment Facts

1 kabob: 205 calories, 2g fat (0 soaked fat), 51mg cholesterol, 50mg sodium, 20g starch (12g sugars, 4g fiber), 29g protein. Diabetic Exchanges: 3 lean meat, 1 starch.

Tomato-Herb Grilled Tilapia

Ingredients

- 1 cup cilantro leaves
- 1 cup parsley leaves
- 2 tablespoons olive oil
- 2 teaspoons lemon zest
- 2 tablespoons lemon juice
- 1 tablespoon gingerroot
- 3/4 teaspoon ocean salt or genuine salt
- 2 cups grape tomatoes, sliced the long way
- 1-1/2 cups crisp or corn (around 8 ounces), defrosted

- 4 tilapia filets (6 ounces each)

Directions

- Spot the initial 6 ingredients in a nourishment processor; add 1/2 teaspoon salt. Pulse until blend is finely cleaved.
- In a bowl, combine tomatoes and corn; mix in 1 tablespoon herb blend and staying salt.
- Spot each filet on a bit of hard core foil (around 12 in. square). Top with herb blend; spoon tomato blend close by fish. Overlay foil around fish and vegetables, fixing firmly.
- Grill covered, covered, over medium-high warmth 6-8 minutes or until fish just starts to chip effectively with a fork. Open foil cautiously to enable steam to get away.

Nutrition Facts

1 serving: 270 calories, 9g fat (2g soaked fat), 83mg cholesterol, 443mg sodium, 15g starch (6g sugars, 3g fiber), 35g protein. Diabetic Exchanges: 5 lean meat, 1-1/2 fat, 1 vegetable, 1/2 starch.

Chili-Rubbed Steak with Black Bean Salad

Ingredients

- 1 hamburger flank steak (1 pound)
- 4 teaspoons chili powder
- 1/2 teaspoon salt
- 1 bundle (8.8 ounces) prepared to-serve browned rice
- 1 can (15 ounces) dark beans
- 1/2 cup salsa verde
- Minced cilantro,

Directions

- Rub steak with chili powder and salt. Barbecue, covered, over medium warmth or cook 4 in. From heat 6-8 minutes on each side or until meat arrives at wanted doneness (for medium-uncommon, a thermometer should peruse 135°; medium, 140°).
- Warmth rice, as indicated by bundle headings. Move rice to a little bowl; mix in beans and salsa. Cut steak , present with bean serving of mixed greens. Whenever wanted, sprinkle with cilantro.

Nutrition Facts

3 ounces cooked meat with 3/4 cup serving of mixed greens: 367 calories, 10g fat (4g saturated fat), 54mg cholesterol, 762mg sodium, 35g starch (2g sugars, 6g fiber), and 29g protein. Diabetic Exchanges: 3 lean meat, 2 starch.

Artichoke Cod with Sun-Dried Tomatoes

Ingredients

- 1 can (14 ounces) quartered water-packed artichoke hearts
- 1/2 cup julienned delicate sun-dried tomatoes (not packed in oil)
- 2 green onions,
- 3 tablespoons olive oil
- 1 garlic clove, minced
- 6 cod filets (6 ounces each)
- 1 teaspoon salt
- 1/2 teaspoon pepper
- Serving of mixed greens and lemon wedges, discretionary

Directions

- Preheat broiler to 400°. In a little bowl, join the initial 5 ingredients; toss to combine.
- Sprinkle the two sides of cod with salt and pepper; place in a 13x9-in. Baking dish covered with cooking shower. Top with artichoke blend.
- Heat, uncovered, 15-20 minutes or until fish starts to chip effectively with a fork. Whenever wanted, serve over greens with lemon wedges.

Nutrition Facts

1 filet with 1/3 cup artichoke blend: 231 calories, 8g fat (1g soaked fat), 65mg cholesterol, 665mg sodium, 9g starch (3g sugars, 2g fiber), 29g protein. Diabetic Exchanges: 4 lean meat, 1-1/2 fat, 1 vegetable.

Salmon Veggie Packets

Ingredients

- 2 tablespoons white wine
- 1 tablespoon olive oil
- 1/4 teaspoon salt
- 1/4 teaspoon pepper
- 2 sweet yellow peppers, julienned
- 2 cups fresh sugar snap peas, cut

SALMON:

- 2 tablespoons white wine
- 1 tablespoon olive oil

- 1 tablespoon lemon zest
- 1/2 teaspoon salt
- 1/4 teaspoon pepper
- 4 salmon filets (6 ounces each)
- 1 lemon, split

Directions

- Preheat oven 400°. Cut four 18x15-in. bits of parchment paper or rock solid foil: overlay each transversely into equal parts, framing a wrinkle. In a large bowl, blend wine, oil, salt and pepper. Add vegetables and toss to cover.
- In a little bowl, blend the initial five salmon ingredients. To collect, expose one bit of material paper; place a salmon filet on one side. Sprinkle with 2 teaspoons wine blend; top with one-fourth of the vegetables.
- Overlap paper over fish and vegetables; crease the open finishes multiple times to seal. Rehash with outstanding parcels. Spot on baking sheets.
- Heat until fish just starts to break with a fork, 12-16 minutes, and opening bundles cautiously to enable steam to get away.
- To serve, squeeze lemon squeeze over vegetables.

Nourishment Facts

1 serving: 400 calories, 23g fat (4g soaked fat), 85mg cholesterol, 535mg sodium, 13g starch (3g sugars, 3g fiber), 32g protein. Diabetic Exchanges: 5 lean meat, 1-1/2 fat, 1 vegetable.

Tomato-Poached Halibut

Ingredients

- 1 tablespoon olive oil
- 2 poblano peppers, finely chopped
- 1 onion, finely chopped
- 1 can (14-1/2 ounces) fire-broiled diced tomatoes, undrained
- 1 can (14-1/2 ounces) no-salt-add diced tomatoes, undrained
- 1/4 cup green olives
- 3 garlic cloves, minced
- 1/4 teaspoon pepper

- 1/8 teaspoon salt
- 4 halibut filets (4 ounces each)
- 1/3 cup chopped fresh cilantro
- 4 lemon wedges
- Dried up whole grain bread, discretionary

Directions

- In a large nonstick skillet, heat oil over medium-high warmth. Add poblano peppers and onion; cook and mix 4-6 minutes or until delicate.
- Mix in tomatoes, olives, garlic, pepper and salt. Heat to the point of boiling. Alter warmth to keep up a delicate stew. Add filets. Cook, covered, 8-10 minutes or until fish just starts to drop effectively with a fork. Sprinkle with cilantro. Present with lemon wedges and, whenever wanted, bread.

Nutrition Facts

1 filet with 1 cup sauce: 224 calories, 7g fat (1g soaked fat), 56mg cholesterol, 651mg sodium, 17g starch (8g sugars, 4g fiber), 24g protein. Diabetic Exchanges: 3 lean meat, 1 starch, 1/2 fat.

Pistachio Salmon

Ingredients

- 1/3 cup pistachios, finely cleaved
- 1/4 cup panko (Japanese) bread crumbs
- 1/4 cup ground Parmesan cheese
- 1 salmon filet (1 pound)
- 1/2 teaspoon salt
- 1/4 teaspoon pepper

Directions

- Preheat stove to 400°. In a shallow bowl, toss pistachios with bread pieces and cheese.

- Spot salmon on a lubed foil-lined 15x10x1-in. container, skin side down; sprinkle with salt and pepper. Top with pistachio blend, squeezing to follow. Prepare, uncovered, until fish just starts to drop effectively with a fork, 15-20 minutes.

Health Tip: Save any remaining pistachios for snacks. A serving (around 50 nuts) packs 6 grams of protein, 3 grams of fiber and more than 10 percent of the B6, thiamine, and copper and phosphorous we need day by day.

Nourishment Facts

3 ounces cooked fish: 269 calories, 17g fat (3g soaked fat), 61mg cholesterol, 497mg sodium, 6g starch (1g sugars, 1g fiber), and 23g protein. Diabetic Exchanges: 3 lean meat, 1 fat, 1/2 starch.

Creamy Lentils with Kale Artichoke Saute

Ingredients

- 1/2 cup dried red lentils, washed and arranged
- 1/4 teaspoon dried oregano
- 1/8 teaspoon pepper
- 1-1/4 cups vegetable stock
- 1/4 teaspoon ocean salt, partitioned
- 1 tablespoon olive oil or grapeseed oil
- 16 cups cleaved fresh kale (around 12 ounces)
- 1 can (14 ounces) water-stuffed artichoke hearts, depleted and cleaved

- 3 garlic cloves, minced
- 1/2 teaspoon Italian seasoning
- 2 tablespoons ground Romano cheese
- 2 cups hot cooked dark colored or basmati rice

Directions

- Spot initial 4 ingredients and 1/8 teaspoon salt in a little pot; heat to the point of boiling. Diminish heat; stew, covered, until lentils are delicate and fluid is nearly ingested, 12-15 minutes. Remove from heat.
- In a 6-qt. stockpot, heat oil over medium warmth. Add kale and staying salt; cook, covered, until kale is withered, 4-5 minutes, mixing incidentally. Add artichoke hearts, garlic and Italian flavoring; cook and mix 3 minutes. Remove from heat; mix in cheese.
- Serve lentils and kale blend over rice.

Test Kitchen tips

- Lentils don't require splashing, however they ought to be flushed and filtered through to search for stones before cooking.
- All things considered, red lentils cook the quickest. Predominantly on the grounds that they're part during handling.
- Since they're part, red lentils separate while cooking and don't hold their shape like dark colored lentils. The

lentil blend turns out to be practically similar to a sauce in this dish.

Nutrition Facts

1 serving: 321 calories, 6g fat (2g soaked fat), 1mg cholesterol, 661mg sodium, 53g starch

(1g sugars, 5g fiber), 15g protein.

Ginger Salmon with Green Beans

Ingredients

- 1/4 cup lemon juice
- 2 tablespoons rice vinegar
- 3 garlic cloves, minced
- 2 teaspoons minced crisp gingerroot
- 2 teaspoons honey
- 1/8 teaspoon salt
- 1/8 teaspoon pepper

- 2 salmon filets (4 ounces each)
- 1 medium lemon, meagerly cut

GREEN BEANS:

- 3/4 pound crisp green beans, trimmed
- 2 tablespoons water
- 2 teaspoons olive oil
- 1/2 cup finely cleaved onion
- 3 garlic cloves, minced
- 1/8 teaspoon salt

Directions

- Preheat broiler to 325°. Blend initial seven ingredients.
- Spot every salmon filet on an 18x12-in. bit of substantial foil; crease up edges of foil to make an edge around the fish. Spoon lemon juice blend over salmon; top with lemon cuts. Cautiously overlap foil around fish, fixing firmly.
- Spot bundles in a 15x10x1-in. skillet. Prepare until fish just starts to piece effectively with a fork, 15-20 minutes. Open foil cautiously to enable steam to get away.
- In the meantime, place green beans, water and oil in a large skillet; heat to the point of boiling. Decrease heat; stew, covered, 5 minutes. Mix in residual ingredients; cook, uncovered, until beans are fresh delicate, blending every so often. Present with salmon.

Nourishment Facts

1 serving: 357 calories, 15g fat (3g soaked fat), 57mg cholesterol, 607mg sodium, 35g starch

(18g sugars, 8g fiber), 24g protein. Diabetic Exchanges: 3 lean meat, 1 starch, 1 vegetable, 1 fat.

Pan-Seared Cod

Ingredients

- 2 cod filets (6 ounces each)
- 1/2 teaspoon salt
- 1/4 teaspoon pepper
- 3 tablespoons olive oil, isolated
- 1/2 large sweet onion, daintily cut
- 1/2 cup dry white wine
- 1/4 cup coarsely sliced fresh cilantro

- 1 tablespoon pine nuts or cut almonds

Directions

- Pat cod dry with paper towels; sprinkle with salt and pepper. In a large nonstick skillet, heat 2 tablespoons oil over medium-high warmth. Dark colored filets gently on the two sides; remove from pan.
- In same skillet, heat remaining oil over medium warmth. Add onion; cook and mix until relaxed, 4-5 minutes. Mix in wine; cook until onion is daintily caramelized, mixing once in a while, 3-4 minutes longer. Return cod to skillet. Decrease warmth to low; cook, covered, until fish just starts to piece effectively with a fork, 2-3 minutes.
- Remove cod from skillet. Mix cilantro and pine nuts into onion; present with fish.

Nutrition Facts

1 filet with 1/4 cup onion blend: 378 calories, 24g fat (3g immersed fat), 65mg cholesterol, 691mg sodium, 8g starch (5g sugars, 1g fiber), 28g protein.

Kale-and-Chickpea Grain Bowl with Avocado Dressing

This veggie-heavy bowl is stacked with crunch and shading, on account of firm carrots and chickpeas, crisp kale, and a lively avocado dressing. It additionally conveys more than 50fi of your day by day portion of fiber, key for weight reduction, vitality, and sound processing. Bulgur, additionally called split wheat, is a snappy cooking whole grain. These dishes would likewise be astounding make-ahead snacks. Pack the avocado blend independently, adding a little water to thin it as required.

Ingredients

- 1 cup bubbling water
- 1/2 cup uncooked bulgur
- 2 (15-oz.) jars unsalted chickpeas, flushed and depleted
- 1 1/2 tablespoons canola oil
- 2 cups finely hacked carrots
- 4 cups sliced lacinato kale
- 1/2 cup vertically cut shallots
- 1/2 cup crisp level leaf parsley leaves
- 3/4 teaspoon genuine salt, separated
- 1/2 teaspoon dark pepper
- 1/2 avocado, peeled and set
- 2 tablespoons extra-virgin olive oil
- 1 tablespoon fresh lemon juice
- 1 tablespoon water
- 1 tablespoon tahini (sesame seed paste), very much mixed
- 1 garlic clove 1/4 teaspoon ground turmeric

Directions

- Combine 1 cup bubbling water and bulgur in a medium bowl. Let stand 10 minutes; channel well.
- Pat chickpeas dry with paper towels. Warmth canola oil in a large skillet over high. Add chickpeas and carrots; cook, blending incidentally, until chickpeas are sautéed, around 6 minutes. Add kale; spread and cook

until kale is somewhat withered and carrots are delicate, around 2 minutes. Add chickpea blend, shallots, parsley, 1/2 teaspoon salt, and pepper to bulgur; toss.

- Procedure avocado, olive oil, juice, 1 tablespoon water, tahini, garlic, turmeric, and staying 1/4 teaspoon salt in a nourishment processor until smooth. Gap bulgur blend among 4 dishes; sprinkle equitably with avocado blend.

Dietary Information

Calories 520 Fat 20g Satfat 2g Unsat 16g Protein 18g Carbohydrates 68g Fiber 16g Sugars 7g Added sugars 0g Sodium 495mg Calcium 26% DV Potassium 26% DV

Quick Chicken Marsala

Marsala cooking wine is a commendable expansion to your pantry; it's dry and sweet without being overwhelming, and can slice through the wealth of cream or stock. The liquor will cook off as the sauce stews. Including spread toward the end, an exemplary system, gives the sauce its body and shine. Serve this skillet primary over polenta, pureed potatoes, or hot cooked darker rice. If you have remaining thyme, have a go at soaking in chicken stock before making a risotto, tossing with cooked vegetables, or adding to a frittata.

Ingredients

- 2 tablespoons olive oil, divided

- (4-oz.) Skinless, boneless chicken bosom cutlets
- 3/4 teaspoon dark pepper, isolated
- 1/2 teaspoon genuine salt, partitioned
- 1 (8-oz.) pkg. button mushrooms
- 4 thyme sprigs
- 1 tablespoon all-purpose flour
- 2/3 cup unsalted chicken stock 2/3 cup Marsala wine
- 2 1/2 tablespoons unsalted margarine
- 1 tablespoon chopped crisp thyme (discretionary)

Directions

- Warmth 1 tablespoon oil in a large nonstick skillet over medium-high. Sprinkle chicken with 1/2 teaspoon pepper and 1/4 teaspoon salt. Add chicken to dish; cook until done, around 4 minutes for every side. Remove chicken from skillet (don't crash dish).
- Add staying 1 tablespoon oil to dish. Add mushrooms and thyme sprigs; cook, blending infrequently, until mushrooms are browned, around 6 minutes. Sprinkle flour over blend; cook, mixing continually, 1 moment.
- Add stock and wine to container; heat to the point of boiling. Cook until marginally thickened, 2 to 3 minutes. Remove skillet from heat. Mix in spread, staying 1/4 teaspoon pepper, and staying 1/4 teaspoon salt. Add chicken to container, going to cover. Dispose of thyme sprigs before serving. Sprinkle with hacked thyme, whenever wanted.

Nourishing Information

Calories 344 Fat 17g Satfat 6g Unsat 9g Protein 28g Carbohydrates 9g Fiber 1g Sugars 7g Added Sugars 0g Sodium 567mg Calcium 19% DV Potassium 16% DV

Shrimp and Leek Spaghetti

Light and lemony, this pasta gives almost 33% of your everyday fiber objective. On account of pre peeled shrimp and solidified peas, it's the exemplification of weeknight-quick. Dress it up with a glass of fresh white wine.

Ingredients

- 8 ounces uncooked whole grain spaghetti
- 1 pound peeled, deveined crude medium shrimp
- 1/2 teaspoon dark pepper
- 3/4 teaspoon fit salt, divided
- 1/2 tablespoons olive oil

- 2 cups cleaved leek (from 1 large leek)
- 1 tablespoon sliced garlic (from 3 garlic cloves)
- 2 cups solidified infant sweet peas (around 9 oz.), defrosted
- 1/4 cup overwhelming cream
- 2 teaspoons lemon
- 2 tablespoons crisp lemon juice
- 2 tablespoons chopped fresh dill

Directions

- Cook pasta as per bundle bearings, overlooking salt and fat. Channel, holding 1/2 cup cooking fluid. Spread pasta to keep warm.
- While pasta cooks, pat shrimp dry with paper towels; season with pepper and 1/4 teaspoon salt. Warmth half of the olive oil in a large nonstick skillet over high. Add shrimp; cook, mixing frequently, until cooked through, 3 to 4 minutes. Move to a plate; spread to keep warm. (Try not to clean skillet off.)
- Lessen warmth to medium-high. Add leek, garlic, remaining oil, and staying 1/2 teaspoon salt. Cook, blending frequently, until leek is marginally delicate, 2 to 3 minutes. Add peas, cream, lemon zest, lemon squeeze, and saved 1/2 cup cooking fluid. Decrease warmth to medium; stew until sauce thickens somewhat, 2 to 3 minutes. Add shrimp to skillet; toss to cover.

- Partition pasta among 4 dishes; top equitably with shrimp and sauce. Sprinkle with dill, and serve right away.

Nutritional Information

Calories 446 Fat 13g Satfat 5g Unsatfat 7g Protein 28g Carbohydrate 59g Fiber 9g Sugar, 8g Added sugars 0g Sodium 649mg Calcium 14% DV Potassium 16% DV

Simple Mediterranean Olive Oil Pasta

Ingredients

- 1 lb thin spaghetti
- 1/2 cup Early Harvest Greek Extra Virgin Olive Oil (or Private Reserve Extra Virgin Olive Oil)
- 4 garlic cloves, squashed
- Salt

- 1 cup sliced fresh parsley
- 12 oz grape tomatoes, divided
- 3 scallions (green onions), top cut, the two whites and greens sliced
- 1 tsp dark pepper
- 6 oz marinated artichoke hearts, depleted
- 1/4 cup set olives, divided
- 1/4 cup crumbled feta cheese, more if you like
- 10–15 crisp basil leaves, torn
- Zest of 1 lemon
- Squashed red pepper drops, discretionary

Directions

- Adhere to bundle guidelines to cook slim spaghetti pasta to still somewhat firm (mine took 6 minutes to cook in a lot of bubbling water with salt and olive oil).
- At the point when pasta is nearly cooked, heat the additional virgin olive oil in an large cast iron skillet over medium warmth. Lower the warmth and add garlic and a touch of salt. Cook for 10 seconds, blending normally. Mix in the parsley, tomatoes and cleaved scallions. Cook over low warmth until simply warmed through, around 30 seconds or thereabouts.
- At the point when the pasta is prepared, remove from heat, channel cooking water and come back to its cooking pot. Pour the warmed olive oil sauce in and

toss to cover altogether. Add dark pepper and toss again to cover.
- Add the rest of the ingredients and toss once again. Serve quickly in pasta bowls, and if you like, top each with more basil leaves and feta. Appreciate!

Homemade Chicken Shawarma

Ingredients

- 3/4 tbsp ground cumin
- 3/4 tbsp turmeric powder
- 3/4 tbsp ground coriander
- 3/4 tbsp garlic powder
- 3/4 tbsp paprika
- 1/2 tsp ground cloves
- 1/2 tsp cayenne pepper, more if you like
- Salt

- 8 boneless, skinless chicken thighs
- 1 large onion, meagerly cut
- 1 large lemon, juice of
- 1/3 cup Private Reserve additional virgin olive oil

To Serve

- 6 pita pockets
- Tahini sauce or Greek Tzatziki sauce
- Child arugula
- 3-fixing Mediterranean Salad
- Pickles or olives (discretionary)

Directions

- In a little bowl, blend the cumin, turmeric, coriander, garlic powder, sweet paprika and cloves. Put aside the shawarma spice blend for the time being.
- Pat the chicken thighs dry and season with salt on the two sides, at that point daintily cut into little scaled down pieces.
- Spot the chicken in an large bowl. Add the shawarma flavors and toss to cover.
- Add the onions, lemon juice and olive oil. Toss everything together once more. Cover and refrigerate for 3 hours or medium-term (If you don't have time, you can cut or skip marinating time)

- At the point when prepared, preheat the broiler to 425 degrees F. Remove the chicken from the ice chest and let it sit in room temperature for a couple of moments.
- Spread the marinated chicken with the onions in a single layer on an large gently oiled preparing sheet dish. Cook for 30 minutes in the 425 degrees F warmed broiler. For an increasingly seared, crispier chicken, move the skillet to the top rack and cook quickly (observe cautiously). Remove from the broiler.
- While the chicken is broiling, set up the pita pockets. Make tahini sauce as indicated by this formula or Tztaziki sauce as per this formula. Make 3-fixing Mediterranean serving of mixed greens as indicated by this formula. Put in a safe spot.
- To serve, open pita pockets up. Spread a little tahini sauce or Tzatziki sauce, add chicken Shawarma, arugula, Mediterranean serving of mixed greens and pickles or olives, if you like. Serve right away!

Greek Tzatziki Sauce Recipe

Ingredients

- 3/4 English cucumber, mostly peeled (striped) and cut
- 1 tsp genuine salt, isolated
- 4 to 5 garlic cloves, peeled, finely ground or minced (you can utilize less if you like)
- 1 tsp white vinegar

- 1 tbsp Early Harvest Greek Extra Virgin Olive Oil
- 2 cups Greek yogurt (I utilized natural fat free Greek yogurt, yet you can utilize 2% or whole milk Greek yogurt, on the off chance that you like)
- 1/4 tsp ground white pepper
- Warm pita bread for serving
- Cut vegetables for serving

Directions

- Prep the cucumber. In a food processor, grind the cucumbers. toss with 1/2 tsp genuine salt. Move to a fine work strainer over a profound bowl to deplete. Spoon the ground cucumber into a cheese fabric or a twofold thickness napkin and crush dry. Put aside quickly.
- In one large blending bowl, place the garlic with staying 1/2 tsp salt, white vinegar, and additional virgin olive oil. Blend to join.
- Add the ground cucumber to the large bowl with the garlic blend. Mix in the yogurt and white pepper. Combine completely. Spread firmly and refrigerate for a few hours.
- At the point when prepared to serve, mix the tzatziki sauce to revive and move to serving bowl, shower with all the more additional virgin olive oil, on the off chance that you like. Add a side of warm pita bread and your preferred vegetables. (Additionally observe notes for more thoughts) Enjoy!

One-pan Mediterranean Baked Halibut Recipe with Vegetables

Ingredients

- For the Sauce:
- Zest of 2 lemons
- Juice of 2 lemons
- 1 cup Private Reserve Greek additional virgin olive oil
- 1/2 tbsp crisply minced garlic

- 2 tsp dill weed
- 1 tsp prepared salt, more for some other time
- 1/2 tsp ground dark pepper
- 1 tsp dried oregano
- 1/2 to 3/4 tsp ground coriander
- For the Fish
- 1 lb crisp green beans
- 1 lb cherry tomatoes
- 1 large yellow onion cut into half moons
- 1/2 lb halibut filet, cut into 1/2-inch pieces

Directions

- Preheat the stove to 425 degrees F.
- In a large blending bowl, whisk the sauce ingredients together. Add the green beans, tomatoes, and onions and toss to cover with the sauce. With an large opened spoon or spatula, move the vegetables to a large preparing sheet (21 x 15 x 1 inch heating sheet, for instance). Hold the vegetables to the other side or one portion of the heating sheet and ensure they are spread out in one layer.
- Presently, add the halibut filet strips to the rest of the sauce, toss to cover. Move the halibut filet to the preparing sheet alongside the vegetables and pour any outstanding sauce on top.
- Daintily sprinkle the halibut and vegetables with somewhat more prepared salt.

- Prepare in 425 degrees F warmed stove for 15 minutes. At that point move the heating sheet to the top broiler rack and sear for an additional 3 minutes or something like that, observing cautiously. The cherry tomatoes should start to fly under the grill.
- At the point when prepared, evacuate the heated halibut and vegetables from the stove. Present with your preferred grain, Lebanese rice, or pasta. It's a good thought to add a generous plate of mixed greens like this Mediterranean Three Bean Salad.

Greek Chicken Souvlaki

Ingredients

For Souvlaki Marinade

- 10 garlic cloves, peeled
- 2 tbsp dried oregano
- 1 tsp dried rosemary
- 1 tsp sweet paprika
- 1 tsp every Kosher salt and dark pepper

- 1/4 cup Private Reserve Greek additional virgin olive oil
- 1/4 cup dry white wine
- Juice of 1 lemon
- 2 bay leaves
- For Chicken
- 2 1/2 lb natural boneless skinless chicken bosom, fat evacuated, cut into 1/2 inch pieces

Pita Fixings

- Greek pita bread
- Tzatziki Sauce (make as indicated by this formula)
- Cut tomato, cucumber, onions, and Kalamata olives
- Thoughts for Sides to Serve Along (discretionary)
- Greek serving of mixed greens
- Simmered Garlic Hummus
- Mezze Platter
- Watermelon and Cucumber Salad

Directions

- Set up the marinade. In the bowl of a little nourishment processor, add garlic, oregano, rosemary, paprika, salt, pepper, olive oil, white wine, and lemon juice (don't add the dried narrows leaves yet). Heartbeat until all around joined.
- Spot chicken in an large bowl and add cove leaves. Top with marinade. Toss to join, ensuring chicken is well-

covered with marinade. Spread firmly and refrigerate for 2 hours or medium-term (see note for snappier marinating alternative.)

- Absorb 10 to 12 wooden sticks water for 30 to 45 minutes or thereabouts. Get ready Tzatziki sauce and different ingredients, and in case you're including Greek plate of mixed greens or different sides, set up those also. (a few sides like simmered garlic hummus may take longer, you can set up those ahead of time).
- At the point when prepared, string marinated chicken pieces through the readied sticks.
- Get ready open air flame broil (or frying pan). Brush grates with a little oil and warmth over medium-high warmth. t. Spot chicken sticks on flame broil (or cook in groups on frying pan) until very browned and inside temperature registers 155° on moment read thermometer. Make certain to turn sticks equally to cook on all sides, around 5 minutes all out. (Change temperature of flame broil if essential). While barbecuing, brush gently with the marinade (at that point dispose of any left marinade).
- Move chicken to serving platter and let rest for 3 minutes. Then, quickly barbecue pita and keep warm.
- Collect barbecued chicken souvlaki pitas. Initially, spread Tzatziki sauce on pita, add chicken pieces (take them off sticks first, obviously) at that point add veggies and olives.

- Discretionary: in the event that you need more things to add to your smorgasbord, think about Greek serving of mixed greens, watermelon serving of mixed greens, simmered garlic hummus, or a major Mezze platter.

Greek Roasted Potatoes

Ingredients

- For Spice Mix
- 1 tsp prepared salt
- 1 tsp dark pepper
- 1 tsp Sweet Paprika
- 1 tsp Organic Rosemary
- For Potatoes
- 4 large heating potatoes, peeled, washed, cut into wedges
- 8 large garlic cloves, cleaved
- 4 tbsp Private Reserve Greek additional virgin olive oil

- 1 lemon, juice of
- 1/4 cup vegetable or chicken soup
- 1/2 cup ground Parmesan cheese
- 1 cup parsley leaves, generally chopped

Directions

- Preheat stove to 400 degrees F.
- In a little bowl, combine flavors. Put in a safe spot.
- Spot potato wedges in a large gently oiled preparing dish (I utilized this one) and sprinkle with the zest blend. Toss potatoes together quickly to uniformly appropriate flavors.
- In a bowl, whisk together cleaved garlic, olive oil, lemon juice and soup. Fill heating dish with potatoes.
- Spread the preparing dish with foil and spot in the 400 degree F-warmed broiler for 40 minutes.
- Remove from stove quickly. Reveal and sprinkle Parmesan cheese on the potato wedges. Come back to stove revealed to broil for another 10-15 minutes or until potatoes are cooked through and have turned a brilliant darker with a little outside layer shaping.
- If necessary, to add more shading, you may put the dish under the grill for 3 minutes or somewhere in the vicinity, observing cautiously.
- Remove from broiler. Embellishment with fresh parsley before serving. Appreciate!

Easy Mediterranean Shrimp Recipe

Ingredients

- 1 Lebanese Rice recipe (or make rice as indicated by bundle), discretionary
- 1/4 lb large shrimp (or prawns), peeled and deveined (whenever solidified, make certain to defrost first)
- 1 tbsp all-purpose flour

- 2 tsp smoked Spanish paprika
- 1/2 tsp each salt and pepper
- 1/2 tsp ground coriander
- 1/4 tsp cayenne
- 1/4 tsp sugar
- 1 tbsp butter (I want to utilize ghee explained margarine)
- 3 tbsp Private Reserve additional virgin olive oil
- 3 shallots (around 3 1/2 ounces), daintily cut
- 4 garlic cloves, chopped
- 1/2 green chime pepper and 1/2 yellow ringer pepper (around 6 ounces altogether), cut
- 1 cup canned diced tomato
- 1/3 cup chicken or vegetable soup
- 2 tbsp dry white wine
- 2 tbsp fresh lemon juice
- 1/3 cup cleaved parsley leaves

Instructions

- To begin with, make Lebanese rice concurring this formula. Leave covered and undisturbed until prepared to serve. On the other hand, you can make darker or white rice as per locally acquired bundle. (Discretionary)

- Pat shrimp dry and spot it in a large bowl. Add flour, smoked paprika, salt and pepper, coriander, cayenne, and sugar. toss until shrimp is well-covered.
- In an large cast iron skillet, liquefy the margarine with the olive oil over medium/medium-high warmth. Add shallots and garlic. Cook for 2-3 minutes, mixing routinely, until fragrant (be certain not to consume the garlic.) Add chime peppers. Cook an additional 4 minutes or somewhere in the vicinity, tossing at times.
- Presently add the shrimp. Cook for 1 to 2 minutes, at that point add the diced tomatoes, stock, white wine and lemon juice. Cook for 5 minutes or so until shrimp turns brilliant orange. At long last, mix in hacked fresh parsley.
- Serve quickly with cooked rice.

Garlic Dijon Chicken

Simple, enhance pressed garlic Dijon chicken is the ideal weeknight meal.

Ingredients

- 1.5 lb boneless, skinless chicken thighs (8 pieces)
- Salt
- 1 large yellow onion, cut into large pieces

- For Garlic Dijon Sauce
- 1/3 cup Private Reserve Greek additional virgin olive oil
- 3 tsp quality Dijon Mustard
- 2 tsp quality nectar
- 6 garlic cloves, minced
- 1 tsp ground coriander
- 3/4 tsp sweet paprika
- 1/2 tsp dark pepper
- 1/2 tsp cayenne pepper (discretionary)
- Pinch salt

Directions

- Preheat broiler to 425 degrees F.
- Remove chicken from the ice chest. Pat dry and season on the two sides with salt. Put in a safe spot for a couple of moments.
- Make the nectar garlic Dijon sauce. In a large bowl, join olive oil, Dijon mustard, nectar, garlic, flavors, and salt. Blend.
- Add chicken to the nectar garlic Dijon sauce. Coat each piece well with the sauce, at that point move chicken to an large gently oiled cast iron skillet (or heating sheet). Pour any Dijon sauce left in bowl on top. Add the onions.

- Prepare in warmed stove for 25 to 30 minutes or until chicken thighs are completely cooked through (interior temperature should enroll 165 degrees F)
- Remove from warmth and enhancement with crisp parsley. Serve hot with Lebanese Rice and stacked Balela plate of mixed greens or this basic 3-fixing Mediterranean serving of mixed greens

Traditional Greek Salad

Description

A genuinely conventional Greek serving of salad recipe is intended to be of not many ingredients: tomatoes, cucumber, green peppers, red onions and feta cheese. A straightforward dressing of amazing additional virgin olive oil and red wine vinegar. Meets up in a short time!

Ingredients

- 4 Medium delicious tomatoes, ideally natural tomatoes

- 1 Cucumber, or 3/4 English (hot house) cucumber liked, incompletely peeled making a striped example
- 1 green ringer pepper, cored
- 1 medium red onion
- Greek set Kalamata olives
- Salt, a pinch
- 4 tbsp quality additional virgin olive oil (I utilized Early Harvest Greek olive oil)
- 1–2 tbsp red wine vinegar
- Squares of Greek feta a great add up just as you would prefer
- 1/2 tbsp quality dried oregano

Directions

- Cut the tomatoes into wedges or large lumps (I cut a few and cut the rest in wedges).
- Cut the somewhat peeled cucumber down the middle length-wise, at that point cut into thick parts (in any event 1/2" in thickness) meagerly cut the chime pepper into rings. Cut the red onion down the middle and meagerly cut into half-moons.
- Spot everything in an large plate of mixed greens dish. Add a good bunch of the pitted kalamata olives.
- Season with salt. Pour the olive oil and red wine vinegar.

- Give everything a delicate prepare to blend; don't over blend, this serving of mixed greens isn't intended to be taken care of something over the top.
- Presently add the feta squares top. Sprinkle the dried oregano.
- Present with dried u bread!

Moroccan Vegetable Tagine

Top pick vegetable tagine recipe! Basic vegetable stew stuffed with the ideal equalization of Moroccan flavors. Veggie lover and Gluten free.

Ingredients

- 1/4 cup Private Reserve additional virgin olive oil, more for some other time
- 2 yellow onions, peeled and cleaved
- 8–10 garlic cloves, peeled and cleaved
- 2 large carrots, peeled and cleaved
- 2 large reddish brown potatoes, peeled and cubed

- 1 large sweet potato, peeled and cubed
- Salt
- 1 tbsp Harissa zest mix
- 1 tsp ground coriander
- 1 tsp ground cinnamon
- 1/2 tsp ground turmeric
- 2 cups canned whole peeled tomatoes
- 1/2 cup storing hacked dried apricot
- 1 quart low-sodium vegetable juices (or soup of your decision)
- 2 cups cooked chickpeas
- 1 lemon, juice of
- Bunch crisp parsley leaves

Directions

- In an large overwhelming pot or Dutch oven, heat olive oil over medium warmth until simply shining. Add onions and increment warmth to medium-high. Saute for 5 minutes, tossing consistently.
- Add garlic and all the sliced veggies. Season with salt and flavors. toss to join.
- Cook for 5 to 7 minutes on medium-high warmth, blending normally with a wooden spoon.
- Add tomatoes, apricot and soup. Season again with only a little run of salt.

- Keep the warmth on medium-high, and cook for 10 minutes. At that point decrease warmth, spread and stew for another 20 to 25 minutes or until veggies are delicate.
- Mix in chickpeas and cook an additional 5 minutes on low heat.
- Mix in lemon juice and crisp parsley. Taste and change flavoring, including increasingly salt or harissa zest mix exactly as you would prefer.
- Move to serving bowls and top each with a liberal sprinkle of Private Reserve additional virgin olive oil. Serve hot with your preferred bread, couscous, or rice. Appreciate!

Mediterranean Watermelon Salad

A simple, crisp and excessively light Mediterranean watermelon serving of mixed greens. Three fundamental ingredients: watermelon, cucumber, and feta cheese. However, to take it to the following level, we add some fresh mint, basil, and a nectar vinaigrette. The ideal dish for your next neighborhood party!

Ingredients

- For the Honey Vinaigrette
- 2 tbsp honey
- 2 tbsp lime juice
- 1 to 2 tbsp quality additional virgin olive oil. Touch of salt
- For the Watermelon Salad
- 1/2 watermelon, peeled, cut into cubes
- 1 English (or Hot House) cucumber, cubed (around 2 cup of cubed cucumbers)
- 15 fresh mint leaves, sliced
- 15 fresh basil leaves, sliced
- 1/2 cup disintegrated feta cheese, more exactly as you would prefer

Directions

- In a little bowl, whisk together the nectar, lime juice, olive oil and spot of salt. Put in a safe spot for a minute.
- In an large bowl or serving platter with sides, combine the watermelon, cucumbers, and fresh herbs.
- Top the watermelon serving of mixed greens with the nectar vinaigrette and tenderly toss to combine. Top with the feta cheese and serve!

Mediterranean Roasted Leg of Lamb

Flavor-stuffed Mediterranean leg of lamb recipe with potatoes!

Ingredients

- 1 4-5 lb leg of sheep, bone in, fat trimmed
- Salt and pepper
- Private Reserve additional virgin olive oil, more for some other time

- 5 garlic cloves, peeled and cut; more for some other time
- 2 cups water
- 8 gold potatoes, peeled and cut into wedges
- 1 yellow onion, peeled and cut into wedges
- 1 tsp paprika
- 1 tsp garlic powder
- 1 Lebanese rice, discretionary
- Crisp parsley for garnish, discretionary
- For the lamb rub:
- 15 garlic cloves, peeled
- 2 tbsp dried oregano
- 2 tbsp dried mint drops
- 1 tbsp paprika
- 1/2 tbsp ground nutmeg
- 1/2 cup olive oil
- 2 lemons,

Directions

- Remove the leg of sheep from the cooler and leave in room temperature for around 60 minutes. Meanwhile, set up the rest of the ingredients and make the sheep rub.
- To make the rub, in a food processor, join the rub ingredients. Mix until smooth. Put in a safe spot (or in the cooler, if getting ready ahead of time).

- At the point when prepared, pat the sheep dry and make a couple of cuts on the two sides. Season with salt and pepper.
- Turn the stove on. The leg of sheep on a wire rack; place the rack on the top stove rack with the goal that it's just a couple of inches from the oven component. Cook for 5-7 minutes on each side or until the leg of sheep is pleasantly burned. Remove from the broiler, at that point alter the stove temperature to 375 degrees F.
- At the point when the sheep is sufficiently cool to deal with, embed the garlic cuts in the cuts you made before. pread the leg of sheep on all sides with the wet rub you made before and place it in a simmering container with an inside rack. Add two cups of water to the base of the cooking dish.
- Season the potato and onion wedges with the paprika, garlic powder and somewhat salt, at that point add them to the dish either side of the sheep.
- Presently tent an large bit of foil over the broiling skillet, at that point place the container on the center rack of the 375 degrees F warmed oven. Broil covered for 60 minutes. Remove the foil and return the broiling skillet to the stove for another 10-15 minutes or until the sheep temperature registers 140 degrees F for medium.
- Remove the container from the broiler and let the leg of sheep rest for in any event 20 minutes before serving.

- If you decide to, halfway through simmering the sheep, cook the rice as per this formula.
- The sheep and potatoes in a large serving platter over a bed of Lebanese rice. Garnish with parsley.

Greek-Style Braised Eggplant Recipe

Top pick braised eggplant recipe, arranged Greek style! Eggplants cooked to smooth delicate flawlessness with chickpeas and tomato. A flawlessly fulfilling meatless supper or side dish. Low-Fat. Veggie lover. Gluten Free.

Ingredients

- 1.5 lb eggplant, cut into cubes
- Salt

- 2 tsp Private Reserve Greek additional virgin olive oil
- 1 large yellow onion, chopped
- 1 green pepper, stem, diced
- 1 carrot, chopped
- 6 large garlic cloves, minced
- 2 dry inlet leaves
- 1 to 1/2 tsp sweet paprika OR smoked paprika
- 1 tsp natural ground coriander
- 1 tsp dry oregano
- 3/4 tsp ground cinnamon
- 1/2 tsp ground turmeric
- 1/2 tsp black pepper
- 1 28-oz can chopped tomato
- 2 15-oz jars chickpeas, save the canning fluid
- Fresh herbs, for example, parsley and mint for garnish

Directions

- Warmth oven to 400 degrees F.
- Spot eggplant solid shapes in a colander over a large bowl over your sink, and sprinkle with salt. Put in a safe spot for 20 minutes or so to enable eggplant to "work out" any harshness. Flush with water and pat dry.
- In a large braiser, heat 1/4 cup additional virgin olive oil over medium-high until gleaming yet not smoking. Add onions, peppers, and hacked carrot. Cook for 2-3

minutes, blending routinely, at that point add garlic, inlet leaf, flavors, and a scramble of salt. Cook one more moment, blending until fragrant.

- Presently add eggplant, sliced tomato, chickpeas, and held chickpea fluid. Mix to join.
- Bring to a moving bubble for 10 minutes or thereabouts. Mix regularly. Remove from stove top, spread and move to broiler.
- Cook in oven for 45 minutes until eggplant is completely cooked through to extremely delicate.(While eggplant is braising, make certain to check a few times to check whether increasingly fluid is required. Provided that this is true, remove from stove quickly and mix in around 1/2 cup of water at once.)
- At the point when eggplant is prepared, remove from stove and add a liberal sprinkle of Private Reserve EVOO, embellish with fresh herbs (parsley or mint). Serve hot or at room temperature with a side of Greek yogurt or even Tzatziki sauce and pita bread.

Kofta Kebabs

An unquestionable requirement attempt genuine Kofta kebab formula: ground beef and lamb blended in with fresh parsley, onions, garlic and Middle Eastern flavors. Add some Mediterranean sides and servings of mixed greens for your next cookout!

Ingredients

- 1 medium yellow onion, quartered
- 2 garlic cloves

- 1 whole bundle parsley, stems removeled (around 2 stuffed cups parsley leaves)
- 1 lb ground beef
- 1/2 lb ground lamb
- 1 cut of bread, toasted
- Salt and pepper
- 1/2 tsp ground allspice
- 1/2 tsp cayenne pepper
- 1/2 tsp ground green cardamom
- 1/2 tsp ground sumac
- 1/2 tsp ground nutmeg
- 1/2 tsp paprika
- Pita bread to serve

For the Fixings:

- Tahini Sauce
- Tomato wedges
- Onion wedges
- More parsley

Directions

- Soak 10 wooden sticks water for around 30 minutes to 60 minutes. Remove from water when you are prepared to start. Softly oil the meshes of a gas flame broil and preheat it to medium-high for around 20 minutes.

- Get ready pita bread and ingredients. In the event that you plan to, make the tahini sauce from this formula. Get ready different sides and plates of mixed greens before you start flame broiling. In a food processor, hack the onion, garlic, and parsley.
- Add the meat, sheep, bread (make certain to press out the water totally), and the flavors. Run the processor until everything is great combined framing a pale meat blend.
- Remove the meat blend from the nourishment processor and spot in a large bowl. Take a fistful part of the meat blend and form it on a wooden stick. Rehash the procedure until you have come up short on meat. For best outcomes, ensure each kofta kebab is around 1 inch in thickness.
- Lay the pierced kofta kebabs on a plate fixed with material paper
- The kofta kebabs on the daintily oiled, warmed gas flame broil. Barbecue on medium-high warmth for 4 minutes on one side, turn over and flame broil for another 3-4 minutes.
- Serve the kofta kebabs promptly with pita bread, tahini and the ingredients you arranged. See recommendations for sides and related plans.

Lebanese Rice

Vegetarian Lebanese rice with vermicelli and pine nuts. An incredible side dish by numerous Mediterranean top picks.

Ingredients

- 2 cups in length grain or medium grain rice
- Water
- 1 cup broken vermicelli pasta
- 2 1/2 tbsp olive oil
- Salt
- 1/2 cup toasted pine nuts

Directions

- Rinse the rice well (a couple of times) at that point place it in a medium bowl and spread with water. Splash for 15 to 20 minutes. Test to check whether you can without much of a stretch break a grain of rice by essentially putting it between your thumb and index finger. Channel well.
- In a medium non-stick cooking pot, heat the olive oil on medium-high. Add the vermicelli and ceaselessly mix. Vermicelli should turn a pleasant brilliant dark colored, yet observe cautiously not to over-darker or consume it (If it consumes, you should discard the vermicelli and begin once again).
- Add the rice and keep on mixing so the rice will be well-covered with the olive oil. Season with salt.
- Presently add 3 1/2 cups of water and heat it to the point of boiling until the water diminishes (see the photograph below). Turn the warmth to low and cover.

- Cook for 15-20 minutes on low. Once completely cooked, turn the warmth off and leave the rice undisturbed in its cooking pot for 10-15 minutes, at that point uncoverand.

Mediterranean Stuffed Peppers

Solid, Mediterranean-style stuffed peppers. The secret is in the rice stuffing with superbly spiced lean ground beef, chickpeas, and fresh parsley. You can even utilize ground turkey or chicken rather, If you like. These stuffed peppers can be set up ahead.

Ingredients

- 2 tsp Private Reserve Greek additional virgin olive oil

- 1 yellow onion, chopped
- 1/2 lb ground beef
- Salt
- pepper
- 1/2 tsp allspice
- 1/2 tsp garlic powder
- 1 cup cooked or canned chickpeas
- 1/2 cup cleaved parsley, more for garnish
- 1 cup short grain rice, absorbed water for 15 minutes, at that point
- 1/2 tsp hot or sweet paprika
- 3 tbsp tomato sauce
- 2 1/4 cup water
- 6 chime peppers, any colors, tops removed, cored
- 3/4 cup chicken soup (or water)

Directions

- In a medium overwhelming pot, heat 1 tbsp of oil. Saute the hacked onions until golden. Presently add the meat and cook medium-high warmth, blending at times, until profoundly sautéed. Season with salt, pepper, allspice and garlic powder. Mix in the chickpeas and cook quickly.
- To a similar pot, presently add the parsley, rice, paprika and tomato sauce; mix to combine. Add the water and bring to a high stew until fluid has diminished by one half.

- Turn the heat to low. Spread and cook for 15-20 minutes or until the rice is completely cooked and no longer hard nor excessively chewy.
- While the rice is cooking, heat a gas barbecue to medium-high. Flame broil the chime peppers for 10-15 minutes, covered. Make certain to turn the peppers once in a while with the goal that all sides get roasted. Remove from the barbecue and let cool quickly.
- Preheat the oven to 350 degrees F.
- Collect the peppers, open-side up, in a preparing dish loaded up with 3/4 cup stock or water. Spoon in the cooked rice blend to stuff every one of the peppers to the extremely top.
- Spread the preparing dish firmly with foil and spot it in the 350 degree F warmed coven. Heat for 20-30 minutes.
- Remove from the oven and trimming with parsley, on the off chance that you like. Serve promptly with your preferred plate of mixed greens and a side of Greek yogurt.

Moroccan Lamb Stew

In case you're hoping to make the best sheep stew, this recipe is all you need! Consoling, self-destruct delicate braised lamb with heaps of veggies, chickpeas and warm Moroccan flavors. You can make this in your stewing pot or weight cooker; directions add for both!

Ingredients

- 2 tsp Private Reserve Greek Extra Virgin Olive Oil
- 1 large yellow onion, chopped
- 3 carrots, cubed

- 6 Yukon gold potatoes (or any little potatoes), peeled, cubed
- 2.5 lb boneless leg of American lamb, fat cut, and cut into 3D squares (Or American sheep shoulder, bones evacuated, fat-cut)
- 3 large garlic cloves, generally chopped
- ½ cup dried apricots
- 1 cinnamon stick
- 1 ½ tsp ground allspice
- 1/2 tsp ras el han out Moroccan flavor mix
- ½ tsp ground ginger
- 6 plum tomatoes from a can, cut in equal parts
- 2 ½ cups low-sodium hamburger juices
- 1 15-oz can chickpeas

Directions

- In an large Dutch broiler (affiliate) or overwhelming stove safe pot, heat 2 tbsp olive oil over medium warmth until shining yet not smoking.
- In the warmed oil, saute the onions, carrots, and potatoes for 4 minutes or something like that. Add the garlic and season with salt and pepper. Remove from the pot and put aside quickly.
- In a similar pot, add more oil if necessary, and profoundly dark colored the sheep on all sides. Season with salt and pepper.

- Go warmth to medium-high and return the sauted vegetables to the pot. Add the dried apricots, cinnamon stick, sound leaf and flavors and mix to cover.
- Add the plum tomatoes and stock and heat everything to the point of boiling for 5 minutes or somewhere in the vicinity.
- Spread the pot and spot in the 350 degrees F warmed stove for 1 ½ hours (check mostly through to add water or soup if necessary). Presently mix in the chickpeas, spread and come back to the broiler for an additional 30 minutes.
- Remove from the stove and serve hot with your decision of Lebanese rice, couscous, pita bread or your preferred natural bread.

How to Make the Best Diner-Style Greek Salad

Ingredients

- 1/4 red onion, daintily sliced
- Juice from 1 large lemon (around 1/4 cup)
- 2 (10-ounce) tomatoes, cut into 1-inch pieces
- 1 English or hothouse cucumber, quartered the long way and sliced into 1/2-inch pieces

- 1/2 head romaine lettuce, coarsely chopped
- 2/3 cup set kalamata olives, divided the long way
- 6 tablespoons Greek Vinaigrette
- 8 to 10 ounces sheep's milk feta cheese, cut into 16 (1/4-inch-thick) cuts
- Dried oregano, for serving

Directions

- Drench the onion cuts in lemon juice: Combine the onion and lemon squeeze in a large bowl and put in a safe spot for 10 minutes. Channel and dispose of the fluid.
- toss the vegetables together: Add the tomato, cucumber, romaine and olives to the onion and toss delicately to combine.
- Toss with vinaigrette: Pour the vinaigrette over the vegetables and toss delicately to cover.
- Serve and finish the serving of mixed greens: Divide the plate of mixed greens among 4 serving of mixed greens plates. Top each plate with 4 pieces of feta and a liberal sprinkling of dried oregano.

Light & Fresh Italian Pasta Salad

Ingredients

- 3 tablespoons olive oil
- 3 tablespoons red wine vinegar, in addition to additional as required
- 1 little clove garlic, minced
- 1/4 teaspoon salt, in addition to additional as required
- Crisply ground dark pepper

- 1 pound dry cavatappi or other short pasta, for example, fusilli or gemelli
- 1 pound fresh bocconcini or ciliegine mozzarella cheese (bite-size mozzarella balls), halved or quartered assuming large
- 1 (8.5-ounce) container oil-stuffed sun-dried tomatoes, depleted and meagerly cut
- 2 medium tomatoes, cored, seeded, and cleaved (around 1 cup)
- 1 (2.5-ounce) can cut dark olives,
- 2 cups gently packed baby arugula

Directions

- Heat a large pot of salted water to the point of boiling. In the interim, place the oil, vinegar, garlic, salt, and a couple of toils of dark pepper in an large bowl and race to join. Put in a safe spot.
- Add the pasta to the water and cook until still somewhat firm, as per bundle bearings. Channel and run quickly under cool water to chill the pasta off. Channel well once more.
- Add the pasta, mozzarella, sun-dried tomatoes, hacked tomatoes, and olives to the bowl of dressing. toss altogether to combine. Let sit 20 minutes, mixing incidentally, to enable the flavors to merge. Overlay in the arugula. Taste and season with progressively salt, pepper, or vinegar as required.

Greek-Style Tuna Salad

Ingredients

- 2 (5-ounce) jars oil-packed tuna, depleted
- 1/2 cup split cherry or grape tomatoes
- 1/2 cup peeled, diced cucumbers
- 1/4 cup hollowed, cleaved kalamata olives
- 2 tablespoons coarsely cleaved crisp oregano leaves
- 2 tablespoons coarsely cleaved crisp parsley leaves
- 2 tablespoons olive oil
- 1 tablespoon lemon juice
- Kosher salt
- Crisply ground black pepper

Instructions

Spot every one of the ingredients in a medium bowl and mix to join. Taste and season with salt and pepper as required.

Baked Red Lentil Falafel Salad

Fixings

For the falafels:

- 1 cup dry split red lentils
- 2 cups approximately stuffed Italian parsley leaves, stems removed
- 2 cups approximately stuffed cilantro leaves, stems removed

- 5 garlic cloves
- 1 red onion
- 1 to 2 serrano peppers, to taste
- 1/2 tablespoons whole sesame seed tahini paste
- 1/2 tablespoons olive oil
- 1 teaspoon salt
- 1 teaspoon ground cumin
- 1 teaspoon ground coriander
- 1/2 teaspoon baking soda
- 1 to 3 tablespoons chickpea flour (or whole spelt/whole wheat/generally useful)
- Olive oil splash

For the tahini dressing:

- 1/3 cup whole sesame seed tahini paste
- Juice of 1 lemon
- 3 tablespoons water
- 1 garlic clove, finely ground
- 1/4 cup minced Italian parsley
- 1/2 teaspoon paprika
- Salt and crisply ground pepper, to taste

For the salad:

- 3 cups shredded lacinato (Tuscan) kale
- 3 carrots, shaved into strips
- 1/4 cup cut red onion

- 3 tablespoons olive oil
- 1 tablespoon lemon juice
- Salt and crisply ground pepper, to taste

Directions

- At the point when prepared to make the falafels, strain and wash the doused lentils. In a food processor, beat the lentils until they are coarsely ground, 3 to multiple times. Add the parsley, cilantro, garlic, onion, and serrano pepper to the bowl, and heartbeat another couple of times. Sprinkle in the tahini glue, olive oil, flavors, salt and pepper, and mix until practically smooth. Make a point not to over mix the blend; despite everything you need some piece. Taste the blend, and alter the flavoring as indicated by your preferring. Add the preparing pop and the chickpea flour. Start by including 1 tablespoon of chickpea flour at once. If the blend is still too liquidy add another. The blend ought to be genuinely sodden, and in the event that you add an excessive amount of flour, the falafels will turn out to be too dry and hard when prepared. I wouldn't add multiple tablespoons.
- Refrigerate blend for 30 minutes. Preheat your oven to 375° F.
- To make the tahini dressing, whisk the tahini glue, lemon juice, water together until rich. Blend in the

ground garlic clove, minced parsley, paprika, and season to taste with salt and pepper.
- Prepare the plate of mixed greens ingredients together.
- Utilizing a tablespoon measure, scoop out 2 tablespoons of the refrigerated falafel blend into the palm of your hand. Fold into a ball a material lined preparing sheet. Rehash with the remainder of the blend. Liberally cover the falafels with olive oil splash and prepare until brilliant dark colored, 18 to 20 minutes. Try not to overcook these — you don't need them to dry out.
- To serve, place the falafels over a bed of kale-carrot serving of mixed greens with a loading spot (or two) of tahini dressing.

Warm Pasta Salad With Tomatoes and Eggplant

Description:

This veggie-pressed magnificence is decent and filling, on account of substantial eggplant. In the event that you can't discover burrata, essentially tear 6 ounces of fresh mozzarella into scaled down pieces. Making a beeline for a potluck? Don't hesitate to make this formula early; simply make certain to let it come to room temperature and toss with an additional sprinkle of vinegar and oil before serving. Add a couple of tablespoons of chopped fresh basil leaves for an additional layer of flavor.

Ingredients

- 8 ounces uncooked casarecce, fusilli, or penne pasta
- 8 ounces haricots verts (French green beans) or yellow wax beans, trimmed
- 1 tablespoon olive oil
- 2 cups chopped Japanese eggplant (from 1 eggplant)
- 1 tablespoon minced garlic
- 2 pt. cherry tomatoes, halved and divided
- 1/4 cup dry white wine
- 2 teaspoons white wine vinegar
- 1/2 teaspoon kosher salt
- 6 ounces burrata
- 2 teaspoons chopped fresh thyme
- 1/2 teaspoon black pepper

Direction

Step 1

- Cook pasta as indicated by package directions,, excluding salt and fat. Add green beans during most recent 3 minutes of cooking. Save 1 cup of the cooking fluid; channel.

Step 2

- Then, heat oil in a large skillet over medium-high. Add eggplant, and cook, mixing sometimes, until delicate, 4 to 5 minutes. Add garlic; cook until fragrant, 1 moment.

Add half of tomatoes; cook until juices begin to release, around 2 to 3 minutes.

Step 3

- Add wine; cook, mixing regularly, until the majority of wine vanishes. Add pasta and beans; toss to combine. Add held pasta cooking fluid, a few tablespoons one after another, if blend is excessively dry. Mix in residual tomatoes, vinegar, and salt. Separation pasta blend among 4 dishes. Top equitably with burrata, thyme, and pepper.

Grilled Heirloom Tomato and Feta Panzanella

Description:

Spring for treasure tomatoes; their rich flavor and dynamic shading add a colossal wow factor to this plate of mixed greens. Beans build it up with fiber and protein.

Ingredients

- 2 pounds heirloom tomatoes, halved
- 4 ounces French bread, cut into 1-inch slices
- 1/4 cup extra-virgin olive oil
- 1 (3-oz.) block feta cheese 1/4 teaspoon kosher salt

- 1/4 teaspoon black pepper
- 1 (14.5-oz.) can unsalted cannellini beans, rinsed and drained
- 1/2 cup thinly sliced red onion
- 1/2 cup chopped fresh basil leaves
- 2 teaspoons red wine vinegar

How to Make It

Step 1

- Warm a barbecue to high (450°F to 550°F). Brush tomatoes and bread with 1 tablespoon oil, and spot tomatoes, bread, and feta on grates; flame broil until roasted on the two sides, 1 to 2 minutes for every side. Move to a plate, and sprinkle equitably with salt and pepper. Let cool 5 minutes; cut bigger tomatoes and bread into chunks.

Step 2

- Combine tomatoes, bread, beans, onion, basil, vinegar, and staying 3 tablespoons oil in a large bowl; tenderly toss. Separation serving of mixed greens among 4 plates; disintegrate feta equally over top. Serve right away.

Zucchini-Pesto-Sausage Pizza

Description:

Prepared to-utilize prebaked outside layers are the key to getting this pizza to the table rapidly. Cut the zucchini and mozzarella as flimsy as conceivable to ensure delicate zucchini and expertly softened cheese in less than 10 minutes. In the event that you like to make your own pizza outside layer and have one available, prebake your covering for around 8 minutes before flipping it over and including the garnishes.

Ingredients

- 3 ounces ground mild Italian turkey sausage
- 1 cup thinly sliced zucchini
- 1/4 cup refrigerated basil pesto, divided
- 1 (12-oz.) pkg. of 3 (7-inch) prebaked pizza crusts (such as Mama Marys)
- 3 ounces fresh mozzarella cheese, very thinly sliced
- 1/8 teaspoon crushed red pepper
- 2 tablespoons fresh basil leaves

How to Make It

Step 1

- Preheat broiler to 450°F.

Step 2

- Heat a little nonstick skillet over medium-high. Add frankfurter, and cook, mixing and separating hotdog with a wooden spoon, until cooked through, 4 to 5 minutes. Move wiener to a plate. Add zucchini and 1 tablespoon pesto to the skillet; cook, blending regularly, until zucchini is marginally delicate, around 3 minutes. Remove from heat.

Step 3

- Pizza coverings on a heating sheet, and spread staying 3 tablespoons pesto uniformly over outside layers. Top outside layers equitably with zucchini blend, wiener, mozzarella, and red pepper. Heat at 450°F until outside layers are crisped on edges and cheese is liquefied, 7 to 8 minutes. Remove from stove, and sprinkle uniformly with basil. Cut every pizza into 4 cuts and serve right away.

Chicken and Cucumber Salad With Parsley Pesto

Description:

This generous dinner salad is a lean-protein powerhouse because of chicken, chickpeas, and edamame; the parsley pesto conveys bone-boosting nutrient K. Get frozen shelled edamame to make this feast additional fast.

Ingredients

- 2 cups packed fresh flat-leaf parsley leaves (from 1 bunch)
- 1 cup fresh baby spinach

- 2 tablespoons fresh lemon juice
- 1 tablespoon toasted pine nuts
- 1 tablespoon grated Parmesan cheese
- 1 medium garlic clove, smashed
- 1 teaspoon kosher salt
- 1/4 teaspoon black pepper
- 1/2 cup extra-virgin olive oil
- 4 cups shredded rotisserie chicken (from 1 chicken)
- 2 cups cooked shelled edamame
- 1 (15-oz.) can unsalted chickpeas, drained and rinsed
- 1 cup chopped English cucumber
- 4 cups loosely packed arugula

How to Make It

Step 1

- Join parsley, spinach, lemon juice, pine nuts, cheese, garlic, salt, and pepper in bowl of a food processor; process until smooth, around 1 moment. With processor running, add oil; process until smooth, around 1 moment.

Step 2

- Mix together chicken, edamame, chickpeas, and cucumber in a large bowl. Add pesto; toss to join.

Step 3

- 2/3 cup arugula in every one of 6 dishes; top each with 1 cup chicken plate of mixed greens blend. Serve right away.

Gnocchi With Spinach and Pepper Sauce

Description:

Our shortcut way form of Spain's beloved romesco sauce brags all the smoky flavor the first with a small amount of the planning time. Gluten Free? We like the cauliflower gnocchi from Trader Joe's.

Ingredients

- 1 (16-oz.) pkg. whole-wheat potato gnocchi
- 1 (5-oz.) pkg. baby spinach

- 1 1/2 ounces Manchego cheese, grated (about 6 Tbsp.)
- 3 tablespoons olive oil
- 1/2 cup jarred roasted red peppers, chopped
- 1/4 cup smoked almonds
- 1 plum tomato, chopped
- 1 baguette slice, torn (about 1/2 oz.)
- 2 tablespoons sherry vinegar
- 1 garlic clove
- 1/2 teaspoon paprika
- 1/4 teaspoon crushed red pepper

How to Make It

Step 1

- Cook gnocchi as per bundle headings, precluding salt and fat. Channel gnocchi; come back to container. Add spinach, 1/4 cup cheese, and 1 tablespoon olive oil; spread and let remain until spinach withers, 2 to 3 minutes. Delicately toss to combine.

Step 2

- Heartbeat red peppers, almonds, tomato, loaf, vinegar, garlic, paprika, squashed red pepper, and staying 2 tablespoons olive oil in a nourishment processor until smooth, around 1 moment.

Step 3

- Separation gnocchi blend among 5 dishes. Top uniformly with sauce and staying 2 tablespoons cheese.

Extra-Crispy Veggie-Packed Pizza

Description:

Our taste analyzers adored this present pizza's crunchy hull and zingy zucchini serving of mixed greens, however the genuine legend was the halloumi—a dry, salty cheese like feta (which you could sub if you can't find halloumi). Sodium amounts shift among brands, so check the label.

Ingredients

- 1 tablespoon white wine vinegar
- 1 tablespoon canola oil
- 1/2 teaspoon kosher salt
- 1/4 teaspoon black pepper
- 1 cup shaved zucchini strips (from 1 zucchini)
- 1 (5-oz.) thin whole-wheat pizza crust (such as 365 Everyday Value)
- 1/4 cup refrigerated basil pesto
- 2 1/2 ounces halloumi or feta cheese, crumbled (about 2/3 cup)
- 2 tomatoes, thinly sliced
- 1/8 teaspoon crushed red pepper
- 1 (2-oz.) pkg. baby spring mix (about 4 cups)
- 1/2 cup thinly sliced red onion
- 1/4 cup chopped fresh basil

How to Make It

Step 1

- Preheat ovento 400°F with stove rack in top position. Mix together vinegar, oil, 1/4 teaspoon salt, and dark pepper in a medium bowl. Mix in zucchini; let remain at room temperature 10 minutes.

Step 2

- Meanwhile, place pizza hull on a heating sheet; spread pesto over outside layer. Sprinkle cheese equitably over pesto, and top with tomatoes and squashed red pepper. Heat on top rack at 400°F until somewhat fresh, around 6 minutes. Go grill to high, and cook until cheese is bubbly, 1 to 2 minutes. Remove from oven, and let cool 2 minutes.

Step 3

- Add infant spring mix, onion, and basil to zucchini blend; toss to combine. Orchestrate serving of mixed greens blend equitably over pizza. Sprinkle with staying 1/4 teaspoon salt. Cut into 8 cuts; serve right away.

Chicken and Bulgur Salad With Peaches

Description:

A quick cooking whole grain, bulgur is ideal for time-crunched weeknight cooking. In the event that you can't discover it on the grains path, you can substitute quinoa or whole wheat couscous.

Ingredients

- 1 1/3 cups water
- 2/3 cup bulgur
- Cooking spray
- 1 pound chicken breast cutlets

- 1 teaspoon kosher salt
- 1/2 teaspoon black pepper 4 cups packed arugula
- 2 cups halved cherry tomatoes
- 2 cups sliced fresh peaches
- 3 tablespoons extra-virgin olive oil
- 2 tablespoons rice vinegar

How to Make It

Step 1

- Bring 1/3 cups water and bulgur to a bubble in a little pan over high. Reduce warmth to medium-low; spread and stew 10 minutes. Channel and flush under chilly water. Channel well; let dry on paper towels.

Step 2

- Meanwhile, heat a flame broil container covered with cooking splash over high. Sprinkle chicken with 1/2 teaspoon salt and pepper. Barbecue chicken, turning every so often, until done, 6 to 7 minutes. Evacuate to a cutting board. Let stand 3 minutes. Cut contrary to what would be expected into strips.

Step 3

- Bulgur, arugula, tomatoes, and peaches in a large bowl. Add staying 1/2 teaspoon salt, oil, and vinegar; toss to cover. Gap blend among 4 plates; top uniformly with chicken

Spring Salad With Herbed Goat Cheese

Description:

Get a full taste of spring with this child spinach, pea, and asparagus plate of mixed greens bested with herbed goat cheese. Whiten the asparagus and peas, make the herbed goat cheese, and whisk together the sprucing as long as 1 day ahead. At the point when you're prepared to serve, toss the spinach and veggies with the dressing, top with the cheese, and supper is prepared. For ease in covering the goat cheese with herbs and cutting it into flawless rounds, make certain to utilize the cling wrap to assist you with moving it and keep it together as you cut.

Ingredients

- 8 cups water
- 8 ounces fresh asparagus, cut into 1-inch pieces (about 1 1/2 cups)
- 1 cup frozen green peas (about 5 oz.)
- 3/4 teaspoon kosher salt
- 1 tablespoon chopped fresh flat-leaf parsley
- 1 tablespoon chopped fresh chives
- 1 (3-oz.) goat cheese log
- 1 teaspoon lime zest
- 2 tablespoons fresh lime juice
- 1 teaspoon whole-grain mustard
- 1 teaspoon honey 1 teaspoon finely chopped fresh mint
- 1/4 teaspoon black pepper 2 1/2 tablespoons olive oil
- 6 ounces fresh baby spinach
- 1 cup thinly sliced radishes (about 3 oz.) 1/4 cup roasted unsalted almonds
- 1 tablespoon fresh mint leaves

How to Make It

Step 1

- Bowl of ice water beside the sink. Heat 8 cups water to the point of boiling in a medium stockpot over high.

Add asparagus and peas, and cook until delicate, 2 to 3 minutes; channel. Dive asparagus and peas into ice shower; channel. Move to a preparing sheet fixed with paper towels to dry; sprinkle with 1/4 teaspoon salt.

Step 2

- 12-inch square of cling wrap on a work surface. Sprinkle parsley and chives in the square. Move goat cheese in herb blend to cover, and move plastic fold over cheese. Delicately fold into a 4-inch-long log. Cut sign into 8 (1/2-inch-thick) adjusts, slicing through the plastic; dispose of plastic.

Step 3

- Whisk together lime zest, juice, mustard, nectar, cleaved mint, pepper, and staying 1/2 teaspoon salt in a medium bowl. Gradually race in oil.

Step 4

- Toss dressing with spinach; add asparagus, peas, and radishes; top with almonds, cheese, and mint leaves.

Printed in Great Britain
by Amazon